"How to" guide

Find the Funds

A new approach to fundraising research

Christopher Carnie

DIRECTORY OF SOCIAL CHANGE   CAF

Published by
The Directory of Social Change
24 Stephenson Way
London NW1 2DP
Tel: 020 7209 5151, fax: 020 7209 5049
e-mail: info@dsc.org.uk
from whom further copies and a full publications list are available

The Directory of Social Change is a Registered Charity no. 800517

ISBN 1 900360 54 3

British Library Cataloguing in Publication Data
A catalogue record for this book is available from the British Library

Cover design by Lenn Darroux
Text designed by Sarah Nicholson
Typeset, printed and bound by Stephen Austin, Hertford

Other Directory of Social Change departments in London:
Courses and Conferences tel: 020 7209 4949
Charity Centre tel: 020 7209 1015
Research tel: 020 7209 4422
Finance and Administration tel: 020 7209 0902

Directory of Social Change Northern Office:
Federation House, Hope Street, Liverpool L1 9BW
Courses and Conferences tel: 0151 708 0117
Research tel: 0151 708 0136

Contents

Acknowledgements

I'd like to thank colleagues in the not-for-profit sector from whom I have learned and on whom I have practised the techniques in this book: my sister-in-law Fiona Carnie, national coordinator of the Human Scale Education Movement and, though she didn't know it, the starting point for my Find the Funds model for fundraising; Jordan for giving me the love this labour required; Psion for inventing the 3a, on which the entire first draft was written; Alison Baxter, my cool, calming, sensible editor at DSC; and a team of volunteer reviewers including Nicola Ramsden and Robin Jones at The Factary, Dr Alison Binns of the Open University, Dr Philip Beresford of *The Sunday Times*, Alison Montgomery of the London Institute, Tony Elischer of Burnett Consulting and Joanna Matthews of YWCA. They have all commented, but the final responsibility for this book rests with me.

Read this quickly

This book answers the 'Where is the money?' question that all fundraisers ask. Starting with the basics I show you how to Find the Funds in the key fundraising markets. In each chapter you will find detailed information about the best places to look – from directories and *Who's Who* to the latest websites and online products.

The focus is on research, finding out and information. We look at using information, managing information, keeping information confidential and managing research. Where appropriate, I have included useful forms and records to help you Find the Funds efficiently. The indexed *Sources list* includes over 120 places where you can find out about funders.

This book tackles fundraising from a completely fresh angle. It is not a book about **how to** fundraise, but a book about **how to find** the funds. I wrote it not for cynical old fundraising hacks but for people like you: bright, innovative people working in not-for-profits of any size. This book shows you how to make fundraising enjoyable again. Forget selling, relationships and all that clobber; when you know how to Find the Funds and you practise Find the Funds, you'll know how to raise the funds. It's as easy as that.

Read this book in any order. It's for dipping into, not ploughing through. And if you've got any comments, views, arguments or suggestions do please let me have them at carnie_jarrett@compuserve.com

Introduction

Why this book?

More people than ever want to find ways of funding their organisation. Most fundraisers in the UK learn **how** to fundraise. But few learn **where** to fundraise. This book shows where, with detailed information about places to look.

And it does more. Only a few people raise funds because they love fundraising. Many are forced to raise funds because it's that or bankruptcy for their organisation. Many of these people simply hate all that selling, all that commercialism, all that 'client orientation' jargon. By focusing on **finding the funds**, rather than on the scary business of **selling the cause**, this book will help these fundraisers find satisfaction and perhaps even enjoyment in their job.

Finding out about donors and 'prospects' (people or organisations that are potential donors or supporters) is easier than you think. The conversational techniques you used this morning at the nursery when you dropped off the kids ('Hi, how's things? Did Christina eat her lunch yesterday?') are precisely the techniques that you need to Find the Funds. Fundraising becomes not a process of forcing your ideas into the minds of reluctant donors, but of asking questions. Loads of questions, directed at collecting key bits of information, will help you feel that the funder is just another human being with interests, thoughts, fears just like yours. Find the Funds is a way of humanising the process of fundraising.

Why now?

This book is needed right now because there is fast growing interest in Britain in research for fundraising but as yet no book aimed at fundraisers that explains the process in a straightforward way. The book you're holding now is here to fill that gap. It's not a simple book but it covers a complex subject in a straightforward way.

But who needs to Find the Funds anyway?

You do! Yes, you sitting there with your feet on the table and a steaming mug of tea in your hand. Why?

- Because it saves time. Find the Funds techniques **save time** by helping you focus on the best donors.

- Because you want your organisation to **look professional** to funders and donors. The Find the Funds techniques explained in this book will help you do that.
- Because good research will gain the **respect** of your colleagues.
- Because if you don't find the funds then **someone else will** – and they will win the fundraising race.

Take a look at any fundraising magazine (or, if you are really keen, read through the Charity Commission's annual report) and you will see that there is a constant growth of new organisations and new people all searching after the same tired old pools of funds. Large companies, big trusts, the rich people featured in *The Sunday Times* Rich List each year: all these are targets of your average Ms or Mr Fundraising.

You can do better than that. With the help of this book you will find funds that most of the rest are overlooking: funds in middle-sized companies; trusts that others haven't unearthed; government agencies with un-pronounceable names; people that have enough personal dosh to keep you afloat for a century. They are out there and this book shows where to find them. Become a skilled fund-finder and your colleagues will start to truly appreciate what you do. I don't want to turn you into the charity equivalent of the school swot, but with the help of this book you will become a **knowledge resource** for your organisation. That will help you to better manage the fundraising process, to ensure that approaches to funders are co-ordinated and thoughtful.

Funders appreciate the time you put into finding out about them. Many hold the view that not-for-profit organisations are amateur collectives of disorganised enthusiasts. You can show them that you are not like that – that you understand the importance of careful preparation and a knowledgeable approach. (This is a theme that many people talk about, but few act on.) There is often enormous pressure from trustees and managers to simply bung out a few hundred letters to trusts listed in an old directory. Resist this pressure (show them this book if it helps) and organise your search for funding.

You probably already spend time finding out about funders. Many fundraisers spend a quarter of their working hours simply looking for information: phoning to check an address, reading through a directory, speaking to someone-who-knows-someone. Disorganised, those hours can be wasted. By organising your research you save time and increase productivity. Simple plans, checklists and techniques such as 'knowledge scouring' (see Chapter 8 *Managing information*) and peer review (see Chapter 4 *People*) will help you do that.

So who's it for?

This book is written for people in UK not-for-profits of all types and sizes – universities, charities, museums, development agencies, associations. Above all it is written for people who are prepared to change their habits, to take a fresh look at the way they think about fundraising, wherever they, or you, may be. It's built on my own experiences as a fundraiser in two middle-sized organisations and in one tiny one, and on years spent at The Factary researching prospects for all sorts of UK not-for-profits. Enjoy it in any order, and excuse me for the awful jokes.

Christopher Carnie

The Factary, Bristol, UK

Limitations, cautions, definitions

Product warning

This book doesn't tell you everything about anything. Here are some of the things it does not cover:

Research outside the UK

This book is limited to UK coverage only. There are other books (check *Targeting the Powerful: International Prospect Research*) in the *Sources list* that give you information about non-UK funders. Within the UK I have taken as broad a view as is practical, so there are plenty of references to Scotland, Wales and Northern Ireland.

Fundraising techniques

As I explain in the *Introduction*, this book is about where to find the funds, not how. There are plenty of good books about the how, including *The Complete Fundraising Handbook*. I am a research extremist on this subject; I reckon that once you know where the funds are and once you have researched them thoroughly, the way you raise funds will occur naturally both to you and the donor. You will simply know so much about them and their interests that a natural marriage of equals will lead to the birth of brilliant fundraising.

Advanced research into wealth

If you are already in the world of share options, investment returns and yacht valuations, then you're going to find my chapter on wealth (Chapter 4 *People*) a little frustrating. This book does not attempt to cover all the research techniques that can be applied to the fascinating business of estimating wealth. I cover the common techniques in ways that make sense for most people in most organisations. If you want more you'll have to ask me nicely.

Funds and stuff

Although the book is called Find the **Funds**, it does cover techniques that will lead you to in-kind gifts. Check Chapter 5 *Companies* for information about this topic.

Use before date

We're producing this book as quickly as possible so that the sources and information don't go out of date. But every day we uncover new places to look, new sources of information about companies, government, people and trusts. In the *Sources list* I have included a number of mega-sites (such as Howard Lake's excellent *Fundraising UK* at www.fundraising.co.uk and The Factary's website at www.factary.com) where new information about sources may be found. I have also shown you the techniques that will help you unearth your own list of new sources. But inevitably between the time I'm writing this and the time you read it some new sources will have appeared and some old ones will have passed away.

More source please, mate

There are over 120 sources, including books, websites and information providers in the *Sources list* at the back of this book. Where a website or publication is listed in the text you will find it in the *Sources list*. Don't go out and buy all this stuff; much of it can be found in a good library or Council for Voluntary Service (CVS).

Jargon

The editor asked me not to use any jargon. But there are two terms you will simply have to learn:

- A **prospect** is a person who is a potential donor or supporter of your organisation or appeal. A prospect may become a donor by making a gift from either their own assets or from those of a company or trust in which they are involved. A prospect may already be a donor (for example Jane Gold is a donor to your direct mail programme but she is a prospect for your new major gift programme). Note the stress on the person: prospects are people.
- **Prospect research** means identifying and characterising prospects one by one. In that way it is different from market research which tries to understand markets (groups of people or organisations).

1

A big new idea: Find the Funds

Find the Funds right through the fundraising cycle

A note on the fundraising cycle

The fundraising cycle, first proposed by Redmond Mullin, is a model for most fundraising:

It starts with the need that you are trying to answer: these children need food; this hospital needs a new spectrometer; this museum needs to organise a conference. The need is the motor that drives the fundraising (for, without a need there would be no requirement to raise funds).

Thinking about the need helps us define the case, the arguments that will be used to persuade people to join us in answering the need. Why is our answer (to the need) the best that can be given? What does our answer do for the people who support it?

The case will be put to potential donors and supporters by our leadership. We need effective, entrepreneurial, visionary, tough leaders who are prepared to give their time to our cause. The difference between a winning campaign and a loser is often to be found in its leadership.

And finally in the cycle, we must find the market – Find the Funds – for our cause. With a clearly defined need, a solid case and good leadership, this is the part of the cycle where dreams are turned into donations and the need is met, for the moment.

Find the Funds and the fundraising cycle

That last part of the cycle is the time when most people would naturally start to look for funding: 'We've got need, case and leaders, now let's go out and find the money'. But just a moment. Have we got the best leaders on our appeal committee or board? Could we find better ones? How could we find them? And what about our case? Are these arguments effective? Will they fit with the ways that funders are thinking?

You can use Find the Fund techniques to help you find new and better people for leadership groups such as your fundraising committee. The techniques I describe in Chapter 4 *People* are as good at finding active people with loads of useful connections as they are at finding wealthy people with open chequebooks. The prospect hypothesis technique, for example, requires you to write out a description of your ideal donor. Substitute 'leader' for donor and you can write a description that should take you to your (future) leader.

The case, as any experienced fundraiser will tell you, depends on who is reading or hearing it. The arguments you would use to squeeze a donation from a toy-boy band are probably a little different from those you would present to Unilever plc. How do you refine, or perhaps re-define, your case to best match the thinking of the reader? You research them, of course. You aim to find out about their interests, their past philanthropy, the people who influence them and their views. Find the Funds techniques such as competitor research (Chapter 3 *Trusts*), peer review and contacts research (Chapter 4 *People*) will all help you to understand your prospect and thus make a really strong case.

Find the Funds fits into three of the four parts of the fundraising cycle. But can it help with the messy, front-line business of really asking for money? Yes it can, and that's the big idea behind this book.

The big new idea?

The big new idea behind this book is that finding the funds doesn't stop at formal research. The same techniques that helped you find that trust or company in the first place can help you right at the climax, the big pitch itself.

Let's listen in to a typical one-to-one pitch:

Martin: 'So, Mrs Poundcoin, we have talked about the World Wide Fund for Sharks and I have explained our work. I have, of course, taken a little time to prepare for this meeting, but I was not able to find out what attracted you to our charity in the first place.'

Mrs P: 'Well, Martin, I read about your Dentists for Sharks project . . . '

Martin: 'But I didn't know you were a dentist!'

Mrs P: 'I'm not, but my late husband, Rich Poundcoin of Poundcoin Industries plc, started his working life as a dental nurse . . . '

Martin, our sensible fundraiser, is finding out about Mrs Poundcoin and her interests before he asks her for a gift. He is researching: in the process of a normal, friendly, enquiring conversation with Mrs Poundcoin he is learning about her motivations, her interest in his organisation. In fact, Martin will try to find out about four key topics:

- motivations;
- assets;
- connections;
- objections.

Motivations

Mrs Poundcoin's motivations are becoming clearer – they are connected to her late husband, Rich. With more gentle questions and conversation, Martin should be able to ascertain whether there are other forces in Mrs Poundcoin's life that would strengthen these motivations.

Assets

Martin will have researched Mrs Poundcoin's financial assets before the meeting. Like all researchers he will have been able to find out only so much. Now, at the meeting, he can use his conversational skill to draw Mrs Poundcoin into this tricky area. We don't want Mrs Poundcoin to show us her bank statements – but we do want her to give us hints and clues that help us decide, with her, what would be an appropriate, stretching, donation for her to make.

Connections

'You should never leave a fundraising meeting with just a cheque,' (not an original Carnie thought; I'm going to credit Tony Elischer with that one). Always look for contacts too. Mrs Poundcoin's friends, neighbours, colleagues and family can all follow the lead that she is about to set. Mrs Poundcoin is the person best placed to introduce these people to you. Of course if you simply arrive at a meeting with a prospect and say 'So, er Mrs Poundcoin, . . . who *do* you know . . . ?' you'll get a blank stare of incomprehension. If you do a wee bit of research first (see Chapter 4 *People* for more on this) you can take along on paper, or even better in your head, a list of people you think she might know, and try them on her. Here's what results:

Martin: 'You know, Mrs Poundcoin, I couldn't help noticing that you used to sit on the board of the Bloater Foundation with Sandy Edges.'

Mrs P: 'Oh yes, Sandy is a darling. Did you know that he's a reformed shark fisherman? As a young man he used to spend his holidays on his boat in the Med chasing the greyfins. Lives just round the corner from me; I see him most weeks.'

Martin: 'That's incredible. I have been wanting to contact him because I'm sure that the Bloater Foundation would be terribly interested in our work.'

Mrs P: 'Why don't I call him now and get him round? And while I think about it, I should speak to Daphne Dangle, you know, the owner of Dangle Baits Ltd. She's made a fair packet out of that little business, I can tell you . . . '

Wonderful things happen when you take the time to unearth contacts. First, your prospect sits up and listens to you in a way that she hasn't before; you have demonstrated that you have taken the time to do some research and that is, frankly, very flattering. Second, she helps you to understand your prospects with information you couldn't get from any other source. Martin wouldn't have found out about Sandy's youthful hobbies except by talking to people like Mrs P. Third, and most valuable of all, people put you in touch with people you might never have otherwise considered. They are simply thinking about their friends in new ways – but you can expect to enlarge your list of researched contacts simply by discussing them with prospects.

Objections

Sales people talk about these the whole time; indeed there are whole sales processes designed around objections. They are the arguments that people use for saying no to a gift, a purchase or a service. Typically they fall into three different types:

- **Delaying:** 'Not this month.' 'Probably best to wait till after the holiday.'
- **Delegating:** 'My accountant/spouse/dog won't let me do that.'

- **Diverting:** 'I'm already committed to RNIB.'

Part of the good researcher's job is to find out what might turn up as an objection, and to have an answer ready.

The **delaying** objection can occur where a prospect is about to go through a significant life change; one major donor I know delayed his gift till his retirement (when he was able to add to it from his golden handshake). Another might want to wait until a share dividend comes in before making the gift. Biographic research (Chapter 4 *People*) and research into shareholdings (Chapter 5 *Companies*) can help you prepare for these objections.

The **delegating** objection is especially common amongst trusts who refer your application to a committee or secretary. This type of delegation doubles your workload, because now you must not only discover the motives and connections of the trust, you must also do the same for its delegate.

We all **divert** all of the time, and often it's our polite way of saying a genuine no. To answer this objection we must understand (i.e. research) the similarities and differences between our organisation and other not-for-profits. We can then talk with the prospect about her/his reasons for supporting the other organisation and look for overlap between our activities and theirs. Mentioning these similarities may encourage a donor to think about your organisation next time.

Martin is good at Finding the Funds. He will carry on researching and listening until he finds the key that will unlock Mrs Poundcoin's gift. And that is the 'big idea'. Simply by taking an interest in people, by researching and asking the right questions we can Find the Funds. Fundraising stops being the scary business of demanding money and becomes the natural process of finding out about a person until you know precisely how their interests mesh with your organisation. At that moment, giving becomes a natural extension of those shared interests.

2

Let's get started

Chapter objectives

▶ Get you started, today, with quick and simple techniques.

▶ Point out the key sources for fundraising research.

▶ Understand the limitations of commonly used information sources.

Let's go!

Here's the proper way to find the funds:

1 Work out what you are raising funds for.
2 Decide which of the many fundraising market segments (UK foundations, large companies, local companies, older women . . .) is your priority group for this appeal.
3 Research these funders in detail.
4 Make a case that is persuasive.
5 Apply to the funder.
6 Receive large cheques.

But life isn't like that. Most of us carry out steps 1–4 in a rush. This chapter is written to help you rush more effectively. Note that all the sources mentioned here are listed in detail in the *Sources list*.

Let us take it that you have a pretty good idea for what you are raising the funds (if not, see Chapter 6 *Feasibility studies*) and that you have decided to aim at prospects in your region. Here's what to do, first with companies, then people, then trusts.

Researching companies – fast

Quickest and easiest sources on companies are:

- *Key British Enterprises*;
- *Kompass*;
- *Yellow Pages* (www.yell.co.uk);
- the Directory of Social Change (DSC) companies guide;

- your friends, colleagues and board.

Bear in mind the pros and cons of each of these sources.

Key British Enterprises

Compiled from the official Register of Companies (held at Companies House), it includes Ltd and plc companies but **not** all such companies, **not** sole traders (John's Fruit Store) and **not** partnerships (Sue, Grabbit and Run, solicitors). For more on these distinctions, see Chapter 5 *Companies*. This directory does **not** include information about charitable giving and sponsorship.

Kompass

This was originally compiled as a guide for buyers – so it has a wonderful index in which you can look up the manufacturers of obscure items such as carbon water filters. That's fun – but it also has a fundraising purpose. When you are running an appeal with a theme (e.g. water supply for rural communities) or looking for sponsorship (e.g. for a swimming event) you can use *Kompass* to identify UK companies making products that fit with your appeal or event.

Yellow Pages

Yellow Pages (www.yell.co.uk) is quick 'n' easy, especially for regional appeals and, again, appeals with a theme.

DSC companies guide

The DSC companies guide follows the DSC philosophy of careful research focused on general not-for-profit use. It is good when you want to make a list of company prospects fast, but like all directories it has limitations. Its coverage largely excludes partnerships and private companies and there is of course a delay between the research and publication – so check the facts before you hand them on.

Your friends, colleagues and board

This is the fastest and best of all – but it needs to be balanced with desk research. Word of mouth information should help you find out about companies that are doing well, and those that are not. I recommend doing some book research first so that you have at least a list of names to discuss with your colleagues. Ways of making this process more productive and more fun are covered in Chapter 8 *Managing information*.

Finding trusts fast

Stretch out from almost any UK fundraiser's desk and chances are your hand will fall on a copy of one of the two big trust guides from either the Charities Aid Foundation or DSC. We will cover these guides in detail in Chapter 3 *Trusts*. Each is available on paper and CD-ROM, each is searchable by name and by trust interest. But bear in mind that these are **not** comprehensive guides; they do not contain every registered grant-making trust (for more on why, see Chapter 3 *Trusts*). So use them, but also, in your rush for some quickie funding, consider using any of the following.

Your database

Most organisations' databases contain, amongst their private, individual donors, the names of some trusts. Sometimes these are only recognised when the cheque, posted by Mrs Smith, but drawn on the account of The Jane Smith Trust, arrives at your accounts department. Search your database for 'Trust', 'trustee', 'charity', 'endowment' and 'foundation', and ask your accounts colleagues about those incoming cheques.

The Charity Commission

The Commission has a website at www.charity-commission.gov.uk where you can check details on trusts for which you have a name, amongst other searches, detailed in Chapter 3 *Trusts*.

Solicitors

If you are doing a regional appeal, phone up solicitors in the region to ask them about trusts; see Chapter 3 *Trusts* for more on this.

Finding people fast

The problem with Britain, as any ex-pat will tell you, is that there are too many people squeezed into too small a space. And people research reflects that. It's easy to find people fast, but you soon end up with too much information about too many prospects. In Chapter 4 *People* I cover techniques that help focus your research on the best prospects.

The two key sources are the leading, original *Who's Who* from A & C Black, and the upstart *People of Today* from Debrett's Peerage Ltd. Both are compiled in the same way. A panel of experts decides who is who, and who is not, and these people are invited to submit autobiographies. The selection varies between the two books, but there is a high degree of overlap between the people listed in *Who's Who* and those in *People of Today*. Business leaders, politicians, leading civil servants, artists, religious leaders, aristocracy, sports people and celebrities all get in there.

The revolution for prospect research came when these two books became available on CD-ROM. We can now search for people interested in a topic (anything from sailing to mushroom hunting) and for people who were born in our region, or a hundred other search topics. How does that help you find the funds? Biographic (people) research finds the people who will lead you to funds: the trustee of a national grant-maker who shares your interest in animals; the director of a leading retailer who shares your religion; the celebrity who has written about learning difficulties in her life.

Suppliers

If you are really rushed off your feet you should consider using a research supplier. Chapter 9 *Finders keepers* gives more details on this topic.

Putting it together

Don't rush the last bit, please. Allow yourself time to prepare a brief, accurate, tidy report and present it well to your managers or trustees. The dangers of getting this wrong are outlined in Chapter 7 *Turning information into useable stuff*.

Steady on

Much research is done at a gallop, with too little time for care or detail. Take a look through the rest of this book and see how a little more time gives substantially better results.

Internet research

Introduction

Don't panic. Internet research is really easy and getting easier. Follow this simple Find the Funds guide, using the wonders of search engines.

Search engines

These are powerful computer-assisted ways of looking through the billions of bits of information in the internet's public face, the world-wide web. Search engines come in two flavours: human and machine. Currently the biggest of the human search engines is Yahoo! (www.yahoo.com). This company employs teams of information scientists to prowl around the web collecting, then classifying, web pages. Their simple classification structure means for example that you can look for 'regions' and within regions look for 'Europe' and within that 'UK' and so on. At each stage you are presented with more sub-classifications, and with a list of web pages that the editors have linked to that topic.

AltaVista (www.altavista.com) is machine-driven. A big computer grinds around the pages of the web, looking for key words. With AltaVista you simply enter the word or phrase you are searching for, in normal English. AltaVista uses clever software that searches for rare words in your request. If you type in 'Find me stuff on Santa Claus in Lapland' AltaVista will focus on the rarest words in that sentence (Lapland, Claus) and search for web pages containing these words. It will display first the pages that contain **all** the words you entered, followed by those containing **most** of the words you entered and so on. Use AltaVista's help section to find ways of focusing your research.

Other search engines opt for one or other, or a combination of these structures; for more examples check the *Sources list* at the back of this book. The human search engines are good for finding background on a topic. Follow their structures and you will find a selection of web pages that match your topic interest. By contrast, AltaVista's rare-word focus makes it especially powerful for finding people's names. Note that none of the search engines cover **all** of the web. Lots of bits of web are simply overlooked.

.com and .co.uk

If you want to find a company's website, try first by going to www.[company name].com (e.g. www.marksandspencer.com) or www.[company name].co.uk. Most large companies now have websites, most of them with an address like this.

3

Trusts

Chapter objectives

▶ Learn about the sources of information on trusts and foundations in the UK.
▶ Find out how and when to use them.
▶ Discover sources you've never used before.

> **Example problem**
> My boss says I should approach the Lucre Trust for a gift. How do I find out about them? How much can they give?

Introduction

Trusts and foundations are a subject for real anoraks like me. There is loads to find out, much more than you can find in your average trust directory. And best of all, they are set up to give away money, so your research should pay off. This chapter covers the ground in three sections. In the first section we look at key sources of information, the second lists other places to look and the third answers some of the common questions about trusts. But first, a blow-by-blow research plan.

Step-by-step

If you have the **name** of a trust and need to know more about it, you should be planning your research like this:

- Check your in-house database and files; collect any information on the trust.
- Visit the Charity Commission website to collect registration information, if your trust is in England or Wales.
- Check the three main directories (see below).
- Phone the trust to request information.
- Check other organisations like yours (see below) for information on past giving.

- Check the file at the Charity Commission for financial information.

If you want to **find a trust that will meet a specific funding need** then your research looks a little different. First you must compile a list of prospects:

- Check your in-house database and files; collect information on trusts that have given to similar projects in the past.
- Use the indexes of the three main guides (see below) to get a quick list.
- Go abroad; check out the guides for Scotland and Northern Ireland (see *Sources list*) for trusts that others will not be approaching.
- Check the annual reports of other organisations like yours for trusts that give to similar causes.
- Use a new-trust source (see below) to add to your directory information.
- Make a list of the trusts you have found, with all their trustees.
- Visit the Charity Commission website, and carry on with the steps outlined in the previous research plan.

These research plans (see Chapter 11 *Finding funds, losing time* for more on this) are basics; for more, especially on ways of making personal contact with trusts, see Chapter 4 *People*.

1 Key trusts sources: England and Wales

The big three directories

The most-used sources are the Charities Aid Foundation's (CAF) *Directory of Grant Making Trusts* and the accompanying *Grantseeker* CD-ROM, the *Top 3000 Charities* from CaritasData and the various Directory of Social Change (DSC) guides to trusts.

These publications are based on different research styles and give differing results as a consequence. Research for CAF's directory, first published in 1968, is centred round a database of trusts. Researchers having once identified a trust then send an outline entry with coded response boxes to the target trust. This has the advantages that it is the trusts themselves who create their entries, and that CAF can deal with a substantial number of trusts. The disadvantages are that a limited amount of detailed information is available for each trust and that a critical research approach is impossible.

CAF's editorial stance (and the appearance of their directories) changed dramatically in 1997 with the advent of a new editorial team. The new team removed a lot of trusts from the 1995 directory because they were judged irrelevant or useless. In fact, many of these trusts turn out to be perfectly OK – so don't throw out those old-style CAF directories.

DSC aims for much more detailed information and a critical analysis of at least the larger trusts. The DSC researchers spend more time pulling and reading trust files in the Charity Commission (see below). This has the advantage that there is more background, more on which to base your proposal, but the disadvantages that only a limited number of trusts can be covered and that indexing of the wordy entries is much more difficult. That's why CAF's indexes are generally better than DSC's.

CAF moved toward the DSC model in 1999 with the *Directory of Grant Making Trusts Volume 3* in which 250 of the major trusts are researched in greater depth. This was a substantial piece of research, involving face-to-face interviews for 107 of the trusts and a mix of telephone and Charity Commission work for the remainder. Future editions of *DGMT* are to be published by DSC on behalf of CAF and are likely to change format again.

The method used by CaritasData for the *Top 3,000 Charities* relies on annual reports for detailed information. CaritasData collects accounts from the leading charities, including both grant-makers and service providers, and analyses the information into a consistent accounting format. Its directory (available on paper and as *The Top 10,000 Charities* CD-ROM) includes charity aims, executives, advisers, detailed accounts and rankings. Its *Who's Who in Charity*, with 50,000 individuals, is based on its database, with additional biographic research.

All of these directories have been helped enormously by the advent of CD-ROM. This allows for much greater flexibility of searching – for example for trustees and for key words – and faster updates. CAF's *Grantseeker* has an in-built expiry date; after that you must buy an update. So far, it has been updated every six months, but Release 3 (March 2000) will not expire until March 2001. From 2001, the CAF and DSC CD-ROMs will be merged to form a single trusts CD-ROM, available via DSC.

The fountain-head

The original source is of course the Charity Commission for England and Wales. Almost all charitable trusts, whether grant-makers (e.g. The Leverhulme Trust), service providers (e.g. a home for older people) or fundraisers (e.g. Oxfam), are recorded here for England and Wales. The exceptions are some churches and higher education institutions.

You can **phone** to check that a trust exists and to get address and registration number information; you can **pay for a printout** of all trusts meeting certain criteria (e.g. trusts with incomes of £250,000 or more that have an area of operation including Devizes). And you can visit their **website** at www.charity-commission.gov.uk, though some of us suspect that the website doesn't report on all registered trusts.

The website includes, alongside publication details, the register of charities for England and Wales. More than 180,000 charities are held in the register and these, of course, include grant-making trusts. You can search the register at the website using charity registration number, charity name, keyword or what the commission calls simply 'area of operation'. These last two need some explaining because they are misleading.

Keyword searches look for either the charity's name or the text of its charitable objects, that is, the objects written when the charity was founded. Understandably some of these objects can be a wee bit out of date. 'Area of operation' means the locations as specified in the original registration document to which grants would be directed. This is not a geographical index of charities by location. For example, a search under 'Gloucester' does not reveal one of the largest grant-making trusts based in that city, the Eveson Charitable Trust. It simply lists charities that, when they were founded, said that they would focus their work on Gloucester.

The real juice, however, is held in the files. Charity Commission files give information on **trustees**, **finances** and sometimes the **recipients of grants**. They list **home addresses** of founder trustees (very useful for new charities) and give you the clearest-ever view of **policy**. I can't show you a file here because the commission won't let punters photocopy them. So order some files in advance and visit one of their three offices (in London, Liverpool and Taunton) to read them. You can order them by fax if you quote the trust's name and registration number. Note that trusts with incomes of £10,000 or less do not have to make an annual return to the commission.

The Charity Commission introduced a new classification system for trusts in April 1997. The revised classification system is based on three areas:

- **beneficiary** – for example individuals, institutions, animals;
- **activity** – for example service provider, grant maker, counselling or advocacy;
- **topic** or field of industry the charity operates in.

At the time when this system was introduced the commission simply swapped old codes, based on the original registration document, for new. This created a mess of out-of-date and inaccurate codes for charities. Searches on the commission's own computers using these codes produce truly awful results. Don't bother, but do look out for a revised coding system from the commission.

Funderfinder

Funderfinder is a useful, low-cost indexing database recording information from the main CAF and DSC publications. Follow a series of questions and menus and Funderfinder will print out a list of trust names and book references for you. The software is available from the Funderfinder website (see *Sources list*) or from your local CVS and is updated twice a year.

Charitable Trusts Reports Service

Smee & Ford's service is based on daily searches through wills that have been granted probate in Great Britain. The Smee & Ford team look for wills that contain a gift that sets up a charitable trust or that substantially adds to an existing trust; around 40–50 are uncovered each year. Subscribers to this service receive a brief report on these wills.

New trusts

We at The Factary claim the credit as the first research team to uncover the potential in newly registered trusts. We first published a report on them in January 1993 and followed up with a monthly report – *New Trust Update*. New *Trust Update* reports each month on 15–18 of the charities registered at the Charity Commission in the previous month.

Nowadays there are others doing similar research:

- *Funding Digest* includes a new trusts supplement;
- *Trust Monitor* includes a mix of recent and longer-established trusts;
- Sunrise Publications list new trusts in *Wealth Watch*.

My advice? Phone the publishers, ask for a sample copy and make up your own mind.

Other guides

Other guides published by CAF and DSC follow the same format as their main directories. CAF's *Focus* guides are drawn from the main trusts database and focus on international work, education, museums and so on. DSC publish local trust guides and information for specific types of fundraising such as *A Guide to Grants for Individuals in Need*.

CAF's **Charitynet** (www.charitynet.org) provides links to other foundation sites, though it can't identify specific foundations for you.

Scotland

There's a wheen o' siller in the bonny, bonny banks of Edinburgh, Glasgow and the rest of Scotland. And some of it is in the accounts of around 3,000 (I'm guessing) Scottish grant-making trusts. I'm guessing because the secrets of all 29,000 registered Scottish charities are locked away inside the Inland Revenue's Scottish Charities Office. Even the influential Scottish Council of Voluntary Organisations couldn't get the safe doors fully open.

But in 1992 they managed to persuade the Inland Revenue to let them have the address details of the then full list of 22,000 not-for-profits. These were mailed with a questionnaire – and the result was a directory of 550 grant-making bodies registered in Scotland (*The Directory of Scottish Grant Making Trusts*). The directory includes financial information, funding restrictions and policy. It does not generally include trustees and many of the trusts refuse to supply full financial data. Another criticism is that the indexing system is too general for accurate application. But it is available as a book and on disk, and there are plans to make it available via a website.

CaritasData have a *Top 1000 Charities in Scotland*, created using the research methods employed for the sister publication featured above. DSC offer a *Guide to Major Trusts Volume 3* including Scotland, Wales and Northern Ireland. The Arts Council of Scotland offer information on trusts for free by phone under their DataTrust service (see *Sources list*). This is a database of 360 trusts and other funders showing policies, eligibility and limited financial information. You simply phone the council and ask for the helpdesk; the service is free.

Northern Ireland

There is no central register for Northern Ireland's charities. Where organisations want charitable recognition, they seek it from the Inland Revenue as in Scotland. The only local information available on Northern Ireland trusts is produced by the Northern Ireland Voluntary Trust (NIVT). Their publication is called *Funding for Voluntary Action* and is available free from NIVT.

There is no one single publication covering all Northern Ireland's not-for-profits, but there are a number of ways to obtain contact information:

- Northern Ireland Council for Voluntary Action (NICVA) holds details of more than 6,000 not-for-profits covering Northern Ireland and the border counties of the Republic of Ireland in their SectorNet database. SectorNet can be accessed via Internet and allows research on a specific issue or a range of geographical searches.

- Charity Choice has a Northern Ireland version of its directory. Details are on their website at www.charitychoice.co.uk
- Bryson House produces a *Social Directory* covering a range of local groups that provide support and self-help on health and social welfare matters.

I am grateful to Nadia Downing of NICVA for supplying much of this information.

Europe

This is a book about Britain but don't forget to check the European Foundation Centre's wobbly *Funders Online* search engine at www.fundersonline.org. A few British grant-makers are listed. For further abroad you could try *Funds Net* (www.fundsnetservices.com) which includes UK listings as well as international lists of trusts and foundations.

2 Other ways of finding trusts

Wealth

It's the rich what set up the foundations, mate, so research designed to find wealthy people should unearth their foundations too. The simple four-step method for doing so goes like this:

1 List interests, clubs and hobbies that relate to your work. If your work involves water cleanliness then list 'swimming' and 'sub-aqua'; if it concerns animals, list 'pets', 'Crufts' and so on.
2 Use a CD-ROM who's who such as *Who's Who* or *People of Today* to search for people who have these interests or connections.
3 Use the same who's who, or a trustee directory such as *Who's Who in Charity* to discover whether these people are trustees.
4 Using the list of names from step 2 above and the Charity Commission website at www.charity-commission.gov.uk look for trusts that have her/his name. This can be a productive way of finding little known trusts. Check trusts with her/his spouse's first name, her/his daughter's name and the house name too. Do not carry out this piece of research for anyone called 'Smith' or 'Jones' unless you like drowning in irrelevant data.

Other organisations like yours

Get the annual reports of a dozen other charities working in the same field. Look at the back of the report for lists of trust donors. Simple as that!

Solicitors

Fundraisers have used old-established firms of solicitors to find trusts, especially when researching for a regional appeal. Phone the firm and say 'I'm trying to find trusts that might support a children's (or whatever) charity. Do you administer any?'

Fundraisers as funders

Remember that many 'fundraising' organisations give out grants. Classic examples are the cancer charities that give away millions in research grants each year. If your project fits with the work of a large fundraiser, do consider applying for a grant. To search in this marketplace, use one of CaritasData's publications which include both traditional grant-making trusts and fundraisers.

Don't forget to phone

Obvious, but after all that searching don't misspell the name of the trust correspondent. Phone to check your research before you send off that grant application.

3 Trust questions and answers

Trusts and money

I hate to mention money in a fundraising book but we had better consider assets, income and gifts. The assets of a trust (which may be property, shares, money on deposit, art) come from the gift of the settlor. S/he may create a gift in her/his lifetime or create a trust from her/his estate. The income of a trust typically comes from:

- dividends from shares;
- interest from money held on deposit;
- rentals from property;
- licensing or other fees (typically those of performers);
- fundraising.

So, dear researcher, you ought to bone up on the financial and property markets. If you are chasing a trust with large property holdings (Henry Smith's Charity has substantial property holdings in Kensington), then it helps to know that rental incomes in London are up or down. This year's giving by Henry Smith's Charity will reflect their income from property rentals. If your target trust is a major shareholder (for example the Kirby Laing Foundation or the Wellcome

Trust) then look at the dividend performance for those shares. Look at Chapter 5 *Companies* for more on these techniques.

How much can it give?

You can use information from shareholding income to help answer our example problem at the start of this chapter. A trust will typically give away the amount it has earned from dividends, rental or other income less any management costs. Some trusts spend their early years building up capital and these, therefore, give away less in that period.

The size of any one gift is hard to estimate but past practice is a good guide. Look at last year's grants as listed in their Charity Commission file, or use competitor research to help you. Phone the trust and ask them what their typical and top grants were last year. Speak to colleagues in other charities and see if there is evidence of steps or limits in donations; in some trusts the administrator has power to give grants up to say £5,000; amounts above that have to go via the board.

The tricky question of past philanthropy

The thing that everyone wants to know, and that is still very difficult to establish, is 'Who have they given to?'. Here are a few suggestions:

- For the larger trusts you can check past copies of DSC guides (you did keep them didn't you?).
- For some trusts you can find lists of grant recipients in their files at the Charity Commission (see above for how to order these).
- Search competitors' annual reports and news from the trade press (*Trust Monitor*, *Third Sector*) and the national press.
- Phone friends in other organisations to see if they have any leads on a trust's past giving.
- Phone the trust and ask them.

These routes should give results for most trusts. The philanthropy of some will remain elusive.

The equally tricky question of future policy

What is going to be next year's policy for the Generously Beneficent Trust? Difficult to answer that one without the aid of a large supply of crystal balls but you could try any of the following:

- Trust policies don't change very fast, so next year's policy is likely to copy this year's.

- Trustees are affected by big social change. The advent of HIV and AIDS, a wave of publicity for domestic violence . . . any of these will move policy toward a new social need.
- Understand the trustees and in many cases you will understand the coming policies. Research each trustee, looking for information that might lead you to guess at their attitudes and motivations. These clues help you judge the likely thinking of the trustees this year and next.

Making connections to a trust

There is lots in Chapter 4 *People* about making connections between your people and the people who run a trust. One technique applies especially to the trust world:

Professional advisers

If your trust is listed in *The Baring Asset Management Top 3,000 Charities* check the professional advisers section of that book. If it isn't, use an annual report from the trust to help you. Now check the lawyers, stockbrokers and so on for your own organisation. Any coincidences? If yes, call up your professional adviser and ask her to help you get an introduction to the target trust.

Exercise

Time for a bit of lateral thinking. Spend an hour at your local reference library with a copy of *Who's Who*, a *Directory of Directors* and this month's editions of your local newspaper. I want you to find information, **any** information, about trusts or trustees **without** touching a trust directory.

Interesting, huh? You probably found a reference to a couple of trusts in your *Who's Who*; a trusteeship listed in the biographic section of *Directory of Directors*; and news relating to one of the trustees of the local community trust in a newspaper search. The idea of course, is to emphasise that there is lots to be found about trusts that is not found in the traditional sources. Use sources imaginatively and you will increase the quantity, the accuracy and the quality of the information you supply.

4

People

Chapter objectives

▶ Understand key techniques in people research.
▶ Learn how to find new donors.
▶ Find donors who can be upgraded to larger gifts.
▶ Discover the networks that link your donors.
▶ Estimate the wealth and giving capacity of your prospects.

Example problems

1 'We're just starting in personal fundraising. Where do we find our first few donors?'
2 'We have a good direct mail campaign. I have lots of £10 gifts. But how can I find five people who can give £10,000?'
3 'I'm organising a fundraising dinner, and want to invite the well-heeled regional crowd. How do I find them?'
4 'Our board needs strengthening with sharp business brains. Where do I find them?'

Introduction

You could write a book on researching people (somebody has; see *Targeting the Powerful* in the *Sources list*.) There is a wide variety of techniques with new methods being uncovered every year.

To make sense of this huge area of work I have organised the chapter into the order in which many people carry out research: starting with people you know (stakeholders) and going on to those you don't. Wealth research techniques are covered in detail.

Stakeholders

The best place to start people research is in your own office. Fundraisers estimate that it costs 15 times as much to recruit a new donor as it does to retain and develop an existing supporter. Even if you are a brand new start-up there are people who can help.

Your stakeholders are those who have a personal or business interest in the continued existence of your organisation. Stakeholders include:

- board members and ex-members;
- clients or users of your service;
- donors;
- employees of the organisation, ex-employees and their families;
- families of clients/users;
- government (local, regional, national);
- members;
- neighbours of the organisation;
- people in other not-for-profit organisations;
- professionals (doctors, lawyers) who advise your clients;
- suppliers (including your accountant, lawyer, bank);
- volunteers and ex-volunteers;
- your bank;
- your founders.

Depending on your specific circumstances you may be able to add to this list.

Exercise

> Make a stakeholders table for your organisation; estimate the numbers in each group; review each group with colleagues to establish why the group is interested in you; and review or research them again (see 'Peer review and 'Wealth' in this chapter) to find the funds in each group. You can use the photocopiable chart in the Appendix.

Stakeholder research helps to generate a list of the people who are closest to the organisation. These people should be amongst your first donors or, at the very least, should be the people who can lead you to your best donors.

Contacts research

Fundraising is a process of moving from supporter A to her friend B, and from B to his friend C and so on to Z. We can use research to accelerate this process and apply the results in many different circumstances: to strengthen our board, to create the personal networks necessary for a capital appeal, to find new donors, to start an organisation from zero.

In each case we start with a name. Let's take a look at Count Lucre's contacts:

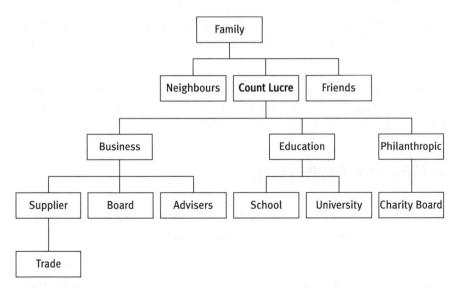

This map shows the main types of contact that a person has. Not everyone has lots of contacts, but most people have contacts of these different types (work, home, church, school . . .).

Each type of contact is researchable. Here is a starter list of places to look:

Charity or trust	*Who's Who in Charity*, *The Directory of Patrons*, Charity Commission
Company board	Directors listings in annual reports, *Key British Enterprises*, *Directory of Directors* or *Corporate Register*
Family	Peer review (see this chapter); *People of Today* or *Who's Who* in their CD-ROM formats; *Burke's Peerage and Baronetage*, *Debrett's Peerage and Baronetage*; genealogical websites
Friends	Peer review (see this chapter), regional or national 'social' magazines (such as *Hello!*)
Neighbours	Electoral register (see note below), your own database
Suppliers	Trade magazines, *Kompass*
University and school	Check the university or school website for alumni information; *People of Today* or *Who's Who* in their CD-ROM formats; university year books

Check the *Sources list* for more!

Notes

The electoral register is available in public libraries. Phone the registration officer for the local council: s/he will often tell you the names of all registered voters at any given address.

People connected to your organisation may well have special types of contacts in addition to those listed here – social services, the synagogue or business school for example. Add these to your contacts map.

Database screening

At present this technique is only cost effective if you already have a list of more than 1,000 donors or supporters. It's designed to find, amongst those supporters, the handful who can give a lot more (see Example Problem 2).

The basic idea is simple: take your database of donors and match it against a database containing people known to be wealthy, well connected and/or influential. At its simplest that can mean checking every record in your database against, say, *Who's Who in Manchester*. One team of scrupulous volunteers, a large room, plenty of coffee and bingo, you find people with influence in your donor database. The high-tech version of the same process involves building or renting a list of wealthy people, then using a computer to merge-purge your donor database against the compiled list; it's a job most commonly done by research agencies.

The keys to this exercise (apart from the coffee) are:

- Before starting, ensure that your data is in good shape. Wherever possible it should include the first names of donors (Christopher L Carnie, rather than C L Carnie).
- Be ready to do more research. The output from a screening exercise requires further work before you can be certain that your 'G Soros' is in fact the billionaire George, not his impoverished namesake Gemima.

Database screening works with donor databases, customer lists or box office schemes. It's best done by computer, but thorough manual screening is almost as effective, especially for smaller organisations. How many prospects will this produce? This depends on your database, your donors and the quality of the compiled wealth data. You can probably expect to find one or two leading prospects per thousand records.

Gold Coast

'Gold Coast' is a wonderful Flemish phrase that describes those parts of town where rich people live. You can use it as a very simple research technique – though it also forms the basis of complex lifestyle and demographic analyses that are beyond the scope of this book.

Let's imagine that you want to raise ten gifts of £5,000 each for your new project in Lincolnshire. You have, as Example Problem 2 said, lots of £10 donors. Ask a colleague who was brought up in Lincolnshire to draw a rough map of the county, and then to mark the areas where the rich live; here the houses have pools and there are two large cars in the drive. Welcome to the Gold Coast. Now use a post code map to convert your colleagues' sketch into a list of Gold Coast postcodes. Find these codes in your database and print out the details of anyone living in a Gold Coast postcode.

OK. It's not rocket science, but it's a simple, proven technique for giving you a first list of prospects who are likely to be better off.

Peer review

Increasingly we are learning to approach prospects personally, face-to-face. Database screening and Gold Coast will tell you who some of the best prospects are, but these techniques will not tell you much about wealth, motivation or contacts.

Use Gold Coast, stakeholders or database screening to create a list of prospects. Print out the names of your best 100 in the first column of a peer review form, and a brief defining note ('Director, Smith & Son Ltd') in the second column:

The Factary Peer Review Form

Name	Notes	Known To	Assets	Motivation	Connection
Jane Example	Director, Example Makers Ltd				
John Sample	Trustee, The Sample Trust				

Peer review is best done with, well, peers – people who know people in the group you are targeting. For a local appeal that might mean your board of trustees, the chair of the chamber of commerce, the director of the CVS and the editor of the local paper. At a national level, and depending on your target group, a review team might include a senior stockbroker, a well connected aristocrat and a leading business woman. In each case their job is to work their way through the list indicating who they know and adding any information they can. The group should focus on the three areas featured in the peer review form: estimating each known prospect's assets, working out their motives and identifying any connections with our organisation.

There are a number of advantages in using peer review:

- It allows you to collect information that is not available from any other source.
- It encourages your peer review group members to suggest people who are not on the list, so adding names to your pool.
- It shows you who knows whom. That information is vital in working out who should ask whom for a gift.
- It works for all sorts of fundraising programmes from huge multinational appeals to local fundraising.

Wealth

Wealth, thank goodness, is a private affair. None of us prospect researchers can ever really know just exactly how rich anyone is. Rightly, their wealth is confidential. But that doesn't stop us trying to estimate wealth. We do so because we want to estimate prospects' giving capacity. We use a combination of three wealth indicators to define a person's wealth:

Assets: shares, property, luxuries.

Income: salary, inheritance, family/legal trusts, property rental.

Spend and philanthropy: what they have purchased or donated.

Assets

To give you an idea of the relative value of different assets look at this table from *Composition of Net Wealth of UK Personal Sector* (Table 5.24, Social Trends 29, Office for National Statistics, © Crown copyright 1999):

Heading	1997
Life assurance % pension funds	36%
Residential buildings net of loans	23%
Securities and shares	17%
Notes, coins and deposits	15%
Other fixed assets	10%
Total (£billion at 1997 prices)	£3,582

The second and third assets in this list are those that are most easily researched and we explain more about this below. These assets are typically also the focus for researchers compiling rich lists.

Rich lists

Various people sell or compile rich lists. In the UK the oldest and best known is Dr Philip Beresford's annual *The Sunday Times* Rich List but many direct mail suppliers can rent you a list of 'millionaires'. Most of these lists use share values or house values as their basis. Philip Beresford's detailed research work is centred largely, though not by any means exclusively, on valuing shares held in public and private companies.

These lists can be useful aids in helping you to estimate wealth. But before you use one make sure you understand precisely how it was compiled, and by whom.

Shares

Share holdings are a relatively easy way of finding out about people's wealth. Remember that companies come in two main flavours: quoted companies, whose shares are traded on the Stock Exchange, and unquoted or private companies whose shares are not (see Chapter 5 *Companies*). If you are working in a regional or local appeal and you want to reach the locally rich you will have to learn about unquoted companies. So take a deep breath and read on.

First, find out whether your prospect is the director of a company. Good sources for this information are *Companies House Online* (www.companies-house.gov.uk), *Directory of Directors*, *DASH*, *Key British Enterprises* or *Price Waterhouse Coopers Corporate Register*. If your prospect is a director then look for the number of shares s/he holds in the company's annual report. Quoted company annual reports are available direct from the company; just phone them up and ask for one. For unquoted companies you must either visit Companies House or request a copy of the annual report by post; in either case there is a small fee for the service.

If the company is quoted, check the share price, today, in the *Financial Times*. Multiply the number of shares held by your prospect by the price and you know the total value of his shares.

Example: quoted company

> Count Lucre is a director of Lucre Industries plc, a quoted company. According to the annual report he owns 100,000 shares in the company. In today's newspaper these are trading at £9.99. So Count Lucre's shareholding is worth:
>
> 100,000 x £9.99 = £999,000

If the company is unquoted you will have to establish the value of the company and, from that, the value of Count Lucre's shareholding. In reality, the value of a company is the amount that someone will pay for it, but we can get an approximation by using the price earnings (P/E) ratio. To be more precise you will have to incorporate balance sheet figures including assets and liabilities.

The P/E ratio divides the share price by the earnings (i.e. profits) per share. These ratios are listed, for most industry sectors, in the FTSE Actuary Shares Indices table in each day's *Financial Times*. For a rough valuation of the company multiply the average of the last three year's profits by the relevant sector's P/E ratio.

To estimate the value of an individual's shareholding you need two more figures: the number of shares she owns and the total number of issued shares. Both of these figures are available from annual report and shareholder documents at Companies House. Divide the company value by the number of issued shares to get an estimated share price. Then multiply that price by the number of shares held by your prospect director.

> **Example: unquoted company**
>
> Frank Luscious is a director of Luscious Services Ltd, an unquoted food retailer. According to the annual report he owns 100 shares in the company out of a total 500 issued shares. The profits for the last three years have been £100,000, £150,000 and £200,000 respectively, making the annual average £150,000. In today's *Financial Times* the P/E ratio for food retail firms is 17.5.
>
> The value of the company is therefore estimated as:
>
> £150,000 x 17.5 =£2,625,000
>
> average profit x P/E ratio = value
>
> Frank owns 100 of 500 issued shares, so his shareholding is worth:£2,625,000 x 100/500 = £525,000
>
> Frank's got just over half a million quid in Luscious shares.

Home

The easiest source of information on house values is the Council Tax banding system. Phone the council that is responsible for the address you are researching and ask which Council Tax band it lies in. Band H properties, the highest taxed, are valued for tax in England and Wales at £320,000 and £212,000 in Scotland.

The other good sources for house value information are estate agents (phone and ask them), *Estates Gazette*, which is now available via the internet, and local contacts who can often describe where the rich areas are in their town/village/county.

Summary

By researching shares and property we can estimate the value of two important assets. Combined with income information, this estimate will help us understand what a prospect can give.

Income

For fundraisers, income is a key indicator of wealth because it means cash money that could be donated. For a minority of prospects, those who are company directors, we can easily identify income; the company annual report gives us a guide either to their specific earnings, or to averages for the directors. Dividends from shareholdings are also calculable from annual report information.

For the rest, rely on two good sources:

- **comparative advertising**: look for job advertisements in the national or regional press offering similar jobs, then check salary and conditions;
- **salary surveys**: there are various salary surveys, some specific to particular industries or trades. For an overview, try *Income Data Services* (see the *Sources list*).

Celebrities

Celebrities, musicians, writers, footballers have other types of asset – patents, licences, copyrights – and you can research these too. A good starting point is a yearbook (of music, football or writing); for example the *Writers' & Artists' Yearbook* lists paperback 'fastsellers' each year, including the total sales volume and the gross income from the sales.

Spend

Luxuries

This is the bit that everyone enjoys, because the key source on wealthy people's spending is, of course, the social and luxury hobby press. Reading *Hello!* and *Yachting World* is thus a **justifiable** part of your work. These magazines often give us a first lead to a rich person. But I am not convinced that they are the best place to look because I'm more interested in people who are making money than people who are spending it. Nevertheless if the work of your organisation can be linked to a hobby that the rich enjoy then you should consider this type of research.

Philanthropy

We can identify wealthy people by looking for philanthropy. A pilot research study by The Factary in 1996 showed that international billionaires donate on average 7% of their reported net wealth to the creation of philanthropic foundations. The equivalent figure for UK millionaires was 0.5% of reported net wealth.

An easy way to do this is to look for trusts or foundations with a living settlor. The best sources are the various trust directories from Directory of Social Change, the Charities Aid Foundation and others, and the Charity Commission (England and Wales) or Inland Revenue in Scotland. For more on this see Chapter 3 *Trusts*.

The annual reports of other organisations like yours may list significant gifts. Make sure you keep up-to-date copies on your bookshelf and collect the names of major donors.

From wealth to gift

How much will a prospect give? There is simply no reliable way of estimating this. The three ingredients we look for are:

- **assets and income**: the subject of much of this chapter;
- **motivation**: interest in our organisation or the type of work we do;
- **connection**: links to our organisation.

It is in the combination of these factors that the gift size is decided.

In order to prioritise lists of prospects, researchers use a simple scoring scheme, applying points in the range 3–1 to assets, motivation and connection (e.g. a very rich person would score 3, a not so rich person 1; someone who was highly motivated toward your cause would score 3 for motivation, someone who was less so would score 1 and so on). The scores are subjective, often based on the results of peer review (see above). By multiplying these scores together you can rank your prospects from best to worst.

And finally, balanced research, please

Let's try to avoid the gender and colour traps. If your research is heavily based on *Who's Who* or a directory of large company directors, chances are that your prospect list is composed largely of 55–65 year-old white men. Balance your research to be more inclusive by using sources focusing on specific populations: *Asian Who's Who International*; *Eastern Eye* newspaper, which publishes an annual Asian Rich List researched by Philip Beresford; *The International Who's Who of Women*; *The National Directory of Black Women's Organisations*; The National Alliance of Women's Organisations and its *News Update* magazine; and, if you can get it, the now out-of-print, *Everywoman Directory*. There is a growing list of directories featuring ethnic minority communities including *Pride of Black British Women*; *E. M. Directory: Commercial and Social Directory of the African, Asian and Caribbean Communities in Britain*; and *Asian Digest* magazine, also from Hansib; the *Jewish Year Book*. Some towns and cities publish directories of businesses led by people from ethnic minorities.

Also, use techniques that are not book or internet based. Peer reviews, connections research and simply interviewing people will often turn up more women and black people than days of searching through web pages or directories.

Conclusion

This chapter has focused hard on the hardest part of people research – wealth and money. Study this stuff closely; it is the key to Finding the (people) Funds.

5

Companies

Chapter objectives
▶ Find out about company types and company language.
▶ Learn about sources on companies.
▶ Learn how to solve a range of fundraising problems using corporate information.

> **Example problems**
> 1 'Companies? I just don't understand them.'
> 2 'Our charity works with lawyers. I'd like to raise funds from law firms; but where do I find out about them?'
> 3 'We get virtually nothing from companies. We'd like to start a sponsorship programme with companies.'
> 4 'We need to find 500 air filters for a project we're running in India.'

Introduction

Just look at the wealth of information available about companies: directories, annual reports, trade journals, whole libraries devoted to the topic. To help you find your way through this info-lake I have divided this chapter into four sections. The first section deals with understanding companies (see Example Problem 1). The second section lists basic places to look. The third covers fundraising problems and how to solve them. I close with a look at more advanced sources and methods, and a glossary of company words.

1 Understanding companies

Company types

In the UK, companies have four common forms: limited liability, partnerships, sole traders and cooperatives. These forms don't refer to size but to the legal status of the company. Limited liability companies are regarded as legal persons; as their name implies their liability is limited to their issued share capital (for help with all these words, see the glossary of company words at the end of this chapter). Partnerships are simply groupings of people working together (in an architects' office or a medical practice); the company is the people. Sole traders (John's Fruit Store, for example) are people trading on their own. Cooperatives are owned by their membership.

Overlaying the limited liability company world is one other key distinction, between quoted and unquoted companies. Quoted companies' shares can be traded on the Stock Exchange. Unquoted companies' shares cannot. Confusingly 'plc's can be either quoted or unquoted, though 'Ltd' companies are invariably unquoted.

Each of these types of company has special characteristics for fundraisers. Local fundraisers do well with sole traders, especially those with a prosperous small business. Partnerships are often difficult to work with because the tax structure makes tax-efficient giving tricky.

Company numbers

There are an estimated 3.7 million active businesses in the UK. Of these, over 2.3 million are sole traders or partners without employees. Only 25,000 are medium sized with 50 to 249 employees and less than 7,000 businesses are large with 250 or more employees. (All figures are from end 1998, reported in the DTI's *Statistical Press Release* of 5 August 1999.)

Quoted companies are the 2,500 or so that trade their shares on the Stock Exchange. Because their shares are traded publicly they are required to make a wide range of information public. This, in turn, explains why the majority of company directories – including those published by the Directory of Social Change (DSC) – focus almost exclusively on quoted companies. Quoted companies are the most common target of fundraising campaigns, but not always the best; by focusing on the quoted companies, fundraisers too often miss out on large or profitable unquoted companies. Amongst these companies and their bosses you will find some of the largest individual gifts to UK not-for-profits. This chapter will help you unearth these gems.

2 Basic places to look

To learn about the corporate world you should take a look at these:

Annual reports	Any quoted company will post you one of these for free, and many are on the internet (try typing www.[company name].com). Unquoted companies reports must be purchased from Companies House (see below).
Commercial reference library	Find the nearest one (most cities have one; ask your local council library service) and spend a morning finding out about their corporate guides. Many also collect the annual reports of local quoted companies.
Corporate Citizen	Published by DSC three times a year and covering the larger, normally quoted, company sector.
DSC directories	The DSC directory (*The Guide to UK Company Giving*) focuses largely on quoted companies. But it does cover corporate philanthropy, something that none of the mainstream corporate directories even glance at. The directory is updated annually and, of course, comes in a CD-ROM version too.
Financial Times	The source of up-to-date information about quoted companies and their people. Reading this daily will give you a good feel for corporate Britain's big issues.
Guides for investors	General investors guides, such as *Investors Chronicle A–Z of Investment*, will help you understand company accounts and the terminology that company people use.
Marketing Week or *Campaign* magazine	On the reading list if you want to reach consumer companies (see Find the Funds for sponsorship below).
The phone	Check company facts with the company concerned; people move frequently between companies and jobs.
The Stock Exchange	(www.stockex.co.uk) has a useful glossary of technical terms relating to shares, and links to share price providers.
Yellow Pages	A free and easy way of making a list of companies in your area or in sectors of interest to you.

3 Answers to some fundraising problems

Let's keep this simple. Find the Funds in companies means finding the profits, so let us try to build a wee list of 100 profitable companies for your appeal.

Profitable reading

Key British Enterprises (KBE) lists 50,000 UK companies (excluding partnerships and sole traders), showing rankings by turnover for a variety of industry groups.

There is a geographic index to help you find local companies and a searchable CD-ROM version.

Dun & Bradstreet, publisher of KBE, is a good source of company rankings. For a fee they will supply on disk or paper a list of companies in any given UK region, showing profits and a variety of other financial information. ICC, a credit-checking agency can supply lists of companies ranked by profits, or you can buy one of their online or CD-ROM products. *Britain's Top Privately Owned Companies* will give you a turnover ranking and profits information.

Ask your local economic development unit (EDU) for their ranking of local companies. Some EDUs publish these as a paper or CD-ROM directory. To find your nearest EDU, speak to your local council or nearest business college. The nearest chamber of commerce is another useful source – speak to their librarian. Chambers of commerce often have standard companies reference works.

From these sources you should be able to build a solid well-founded list of the 100 most profitable companies for your appeal. But your list will contain some gaps: specifically, it will not contain partnerships, nor will it contain sole traders.

Finding partnerships

To add partnerships to your list of 100 you will have to get specific, looking in detail industry by industry.

Accountants, surveyors, lawyers

Accountants are listed in *Tuckers' Directory of the Accountants 500* and surveyors in the similar *Tuckers' Directory of the Surveyors 500*. Both books are a mix of facts (number of partners) and estimates (turnover and profits) because financial information on partnerships is so hard to find. *Chambers Directory* offers at their website a free searchable database of leading firms of solicitors and barristers. The site includes regional listings and a top 50 ranking. *Havers Companion to the Bar* does the same job in paper form.

Note that many partnerships are transforming themselves into limited companies – incorporating to limit their liabilities – so more information on this relatively hidden group of companies should become available soon.

Other partnerships

Speak to the relevant trade association or even better, arrange to visit their library. Trade magazines will sometimes publish rankings; if you have the budget use some of the suppliers listed in the fourth section of this chapter, Getting in deep, to search the trade press.

Finding sole traders

Profitability-based rankings simply don't exist for this group (go on, prove me wrong). Local enterprise agencies and chambers of commerce may supply information, but as good a source as any is simply to walk your local streets, noting down shops and traders.

Finding the philanthropists

Corporate philanthropy and community investment is not the subject of much coverage, despite the interest it generates amongst fundraisers. The DSC guides do an honourable job, but their coverage is necessarily national and centred on the quoted company market. CaritasData's *Top 3,000 Charities* lists companies and their gifts to charity, using corporate annual reports as the source.

One obvious route is to check whether the company has an associated trust or foundation; for UK national firms try the Charities Aid Foundation or Directory of Social Change trust guides (see Chapter 3 *Trusts*), or the Charity Commission website. Bear in mind that these corporate trusts, though legally separate from the company, are normally linked to the founding company's interests.

There are a few corporate responsibility networks, such as Business in the Community, which publish lists of members. An international example is Social Venture Network Europe (SVN, www.svneurope.com/index.html). This is an association of companies and individual business leaders who, say SVN, 'believe they can – and must – make a significant contribution to solve social and environmental problems locally and globally'.

You can find lists of companies that support other organisations like yours in those organisations' annual reports. And of course you could just talk to the companies themselves (though you may find that companies outside the top 2,000 simply do not have any idea of community or charitable policies). For larger companies, speak to the corporate community affairs manager. For smaller or unquoted companies, aim for the chair or managing director, or her/his assistant. For middle-sized companies especially it is often the leadership who decide on philanthropy. So use the people research techniques outlined in Chapter 4 *People* to understand the person in the chair.

Find the Funds for sponsorship

The needs and often the mindset of people working in sponsorship, cause-related marketing and sales promotions are very different from the rest of the fundraising world. Enough of all that pleading for donations; let's sell!

Research has to move up a gear too. The focus is on marketing and selling in the corporate world, so start by reading and clipping the key general magazines in this world – *Campaign* and *PR Week*. Here you will find new product announcements and rumours (a good time for a joint promotion), tables of sales by value and key people. You will also find information about the marketing, advertising and PR agencies that supply companies. These agencies are vital intermediaries in the sponsorship world and can help you make your case to their clients. For more on these client–agency relationships try *Hollis UK Press and Public Relations Annual*, which lists companies and their PR agencies, or *BRAD*, which lists agencies, brand names and brand owners.

Trade exhibition catalogues list products and often name the brand-manager or marketing manager; check www.expoguide.com for a list of current or relevant exhibitions, trade shows and conferences.

The best quality information for sponsorship comes from trade journalists. These people know their industry and the people leading it. Find them in the trade press and via the *World Guide to Trade Associations*. For other specialists in a given sector or problem you can try the *UK Register of Expert Witnesses* which includes indexed biographies of people reckoned to be experts in defined fields.

Find the Funds in sponsorship: a worked example

Nicola is a typical one-person fundraiser. She works for an organisation that provides clean water boreholes in the developing world. She must find the funds, get the gifts and make the coffee. Nicola has no time for all this research stuff. But she desperately needs a sponsor.

So she concentrates on finding the largest companies in the water-pumping industries. Here the directories are useful. Nicola uses *Kompass* to find companies in the right sector and uses *Key British Enterprises* to confirm the *Kompass* information. She looks for turnover (i.e. sales) and does a simple ranking of the top 30 companies in the sector. In each case she records the names of the chair or president and the marketing director. Now she has a first list.

She turns to the trade journal, *Heating and Plumbing Monthly*, for the last three months and looks for hot news about these companies. She notes changes in key personnel, links with PR agencies and new products. She bones up on competition and key trends in the sector. She photocopies any in-depth profiles of either leading companies or people.

Nicola now uses *Who's Who*, *People of Today* and *Directory of Directors* to collect biographies of any of the leading people in the sector. (It has helped that she stored the company director information alphabetically by surname.) In the biographic sources she looks for any links with not-for-profits.

Nicola has used sources efficiently to get just what she wants – a list of the top 30 companies and their leaders, with up-to-date news. Next step is to boost her understanding with personal knowledge by discussing the industry and its future with a friend who is the PR director of a medium-sized copper-pipe manufacturer.

Cleverly, Nicola now checks in house. She starts with her database, looking for any past contact with the industry leaders uncovered in her library research; then she speaks to her board to find out if anyone knows any of these key door-openers. (For more on these techniques, see Chapter 4 *People*.)

Nicola has done a thorough, focused, fast research job on the sector. Eight hours after she started she has valuable information about 30 companies and has identified five real prospects for her sponsorship programme.

Find an in-kind gift

Kompass was originally created for buyers. Want to buy a 15mm left-threaded stainless steel bolt? *Kompass* has a products guide that will help you locate the three manufacturers in the UK who make them. This makes *Kompass* invaluable when you want to find an in-kind donor. Using the detailed products index you can find all the companies that manufacture the in-kind gift you want. In a separate companies section (in the paper version) are company details including directors names, financials, products list and regional office locations.

Kompass is available online at ReedBase (see *Sources list*). This database also contains information from *Kelly's Directory*, *Dial Industry* and *Directory of Directors*. It profiles 1.5m companies world-wide, of which 200,000 are in the UK. Company profiles include financial information, acquisitions and recent news. The database is updated daily – about 1,500 updates are made each day, the company claims.

Other good places to look:

- Gifts In Kind UK, a charity 'broker' for gifts in kind;

- trade associations, especially their libraries;
- trade press;
- exhibition catalogues (try Expoguide for a list of current and relevant events).

Find the employee funders

Give as you earn is a small but growing sector of fundraising, and Charities Aid Foundation can help you find out about the companies which are involved. Their website, www.giveasyouearn.org, includes a 'Contracted employer' list that is available for download at no cost. Bear in mind that company employees support charities in lots of different ways, from give as you earn to charity adoption and fundraising events.

4 Getting in deep

I started this chapter by saying that there is too much information about companies. For some people this information is crucial in helping them make the most of their corporate fundraising. Here then is the Corporate Anorak's Compendium:

Companies House

Companies House Direct is the online service for the Register of Companies. It's the easiest way of accessing their services, which remain available for personal callers and postal enquiries to their offices. The register is the place where all Britain's 1.2 million limited liability companies (and a few more obscure types too) are recorded. With the name, or even better the registered number of the company (the registered number is printed on their letterhead and annual report) you can find financial, debt, directorship and share ownership information.

An advantage of the online version is that it is easy to search for company directors. Once you have found Lucy Blenkinsop Luscious, Companies House online displays all her directorships and her home address (allowing you to confirm that the L B Luscious in your donor database is in fact a valuable corporate contact into Luscious Industries plc).

Dialog

The Dialog Corporation hosts the Rolls-Royce of corporate databases. Previously known as Maid, Corporate Profound, Knight-Ridder and Datastar, Dialog offers a bewildering variety of corporate information including many of the big name directories and information providers (Economist Intelligence

Unit, Mintel, Datamonitor, Reuters). There is news, directories, analysts' reports, trade journals, specialist newsletters. It includes UK government and European Community press releases, handbooks and encyclopaedias. Dialog can be paid for either as a simple credit card transaction or as a subscriber service; the price reflects the huge volume of high quality information that the service offers, and a reputation for good customer support and training.

Note that some Dialog files are available on a pay-per-view basis through secondary providers such as Compuserve.

FT Profile

If you simply want a searchable database of company news then try FT Profile. It has comprehensive coverage of UK national and regional press, specialist magazines and trade press. FT Profile is one of many databases that allow you to search for any mention of the company or topic you are researching, in the text of hundreds of publications. This allows you to be bang up to date with your corporate information.

UK Equities

UK Equities Direct publishes financial data on quoted UK companies, including the names of directors. This service is still free as I write but, like many web-based services, is likely to introduce charges in the future.

DASH

DASH, from Dun & Bradstreet and Bureau van Dijk, has become an invaluable research tool for those who can get it. It's a CD containing details of 400,000 primary companies and their one million directors and 650,000 secondary companies and their 820,000 directors. You can search for company details, select companies by address, trade and financial data, identify company directors and shareholders, and find all the directorships of any director.

Ethics and risk assessment

The full scope of ethical research is beyond the scope of this book because the searches that are required depend heavily on the particular ethical constraints of the organisation concerned. I prefer to call this area 'risk assessment' because it often goes beyond morals and ethics and into an examination of whether or not association carries any risks for us, the not-for-profit. Here are some tips to help you with this area:

- Clarify precisely which ethical limits you want to set. Alcohol? Armaments? Gambling? Pollutant chemicals? For each topic, set guidelines that are capable of being researched, for example: no more than 10% of the company's turnover must arise from the manufacture of alcoholic drinks.
- Use the annual report and trade press as initial sources.
- Check for membership of one of the networks of corporate social responsibility (see 'Finding the philanthropists' above).
- Seek advice from one of the campaigning organisations (Greenpeace, Campaign Against the Arms Trade) to help you decide which companies are outside your ethical limit.

EIRIS, the Ethical Investors Research Service, offers help to put ethical principles into practice. EIRIS provides independent research into corporate behaviour and helps charities and other investors identify appropriate companies for investment and fundraising; they also publish newsletters on corporate ethics and investment. At present EIRIS covers around 1,500 companies, of which 350 are in continental Europe.

A company profile

If you are planning to research more than a handful of companies, create a blank standard profile for doing so. There is an example for you to use in the Appendix. Sources of information for each of the elements of your profile are detailed in this chapter.

With a standard profile, you know exactly what to find out – and what to omit. Because there is far more information about most companies than you are ever likely to want, standard profiles save research time and help ensure that the right information flows out of your organisation.

Glossary of company words

Some of the common words and their definitions are:

CCI	Corporate community investment: staff, products and other resources from the company for the benefit of the local community.
Close company	A UK company which is controlled by not more than five shareholders or their families or partners.
CRM	Cause related marketing: linking the brand and image of a good cause to the marketing of a product. Normally paid for from marketing budgets.

Gearing	The proportion of capital employed of a company that is financed by lenders rather than shareholders.
Incentive shares	Share options (q.v.) as an incentive for employees to increase the share price.
Net current assets	An alternative name for working capital, i.e. the current assets less current liabilities.
Partnership	A company run by a group of sole traders, with unlimited liability.
Private company	A company that is not allowed to issue shares or loan stock to the public.
Public company	A company whose shares and loan stock may be publicly traded. A public company must have plc as part of its name
Quoted company	Means the same as a public company.
Retained profits	Profits that have not been paid out as dividends to shareholders.
Rights issue	The issue of new shares by a company to existing shareholders.
Share capital	The nominal value of the shares that have been issued by a company.
Share options	The right to purchase shares at a set price on a set future date.
Sole trader	A company run by one person, with unlimited liability.
Turnover	The sales revenue of an accounting period.

The state

This book is primarily about private sector funding. There are others that cover state funding (from UK, national, regional or local government sources, quangos and other intermediaries) in detail, and it is not my job to repeat what they say. Instead, here are a few pointers to help you research state funding.

- Speak to people in other similar organisations. People in charities are generally very helpful and generous with their time and their knowledge. Ask about local or regional funding opportunities.
- Understand the structures. The structures of government can be complex, but to find the funds you will have to unravel them. Use the resources of your local reference library, the *Civil Service Yearbook* and its website, and the librarians and information people listed in *Guide to Libraries and Information Units in Government Departments and other Organisations.* The *Civil Service Yearbook* website is a wonder, with clear descriptions of how each department is organised and their links to executive agencies.
- Many government departments have delegated voluntary sector liaison officers who can supply lists of contacts in their department relevant to you, the grant-seeker.
- Many departments have information officers whose job it is to help you find your way in their department. Use them.
- Work methodically through each section of the executive structure. Look within the department or executive agency for sections that might be relevant to your problem. Speak to all of these sections to find out about current and planned grant aid.
- Interview elected members. Visit your MP's surgery, or meet up with your local councillor. Members can ask questions of the administration (the civil service) that will help to uncover funding.
- Read departments' and councils' annual reports. These cover, in detail, the expenditure of each department including their grant programmes.
- Ask for departments' guides to voluntary sector funding.
- Check the Vacher and Vacher Dod guides; these help you understand the connections between the civil service and MPs.

With thanks to Susan Forrester, whose book *A Guide to Funding from Government Departments and Agencies* is a vital research source for this form of fundraising.

6

Feasibility studies

Chapter objectives

▶ Learn how to carry out a feasibility study for a small to medium-sized project.
▶ Learn how to use modern research techniques in a feasibility study.

> **Example problem**
>
> 'We want to raise funds for a new day centre, but we just don't know if it's feasible. We spoke to a few consultants about a feasibility study but they all seem to cost so much. Can't we do it ourselves?'

Why study feasibility?

We study feasibility to:

- reduce risk;
- convince our board;
- discover new directions;
- identify donors;
- find out what it is about our work that interests people.

A feasibility study takes time, but it can save a lot of wasted effort. The hours you invest in a study are hours invested in risk-reduction, saving much wasted effort later. By planning a study carefully, and by using the research techniques we describe here, you can keep your investment of hours to a minimum. And feasibility studies bring all sorts of other benefits. You are sure to learn lots that you didn't know about your donors. You are pretty likely to learn lots about your organisation and its people too.

When should we do a study?

In the business world this type of study is used regularly before a new product is launched or considered. The same should apply in the not-for-profit sector; whenever we are considering a new fundraising programme, a new way of promoting legacies, a significant change in direction, we should study the feasibility of our idea beforehand.

Find the Funds

To understand whether our project is feasible we need to find out where the funds are. Where is the money in your region or work area?

As you know, there are four main 'markets' in fundraising: government/state; people; grant-making trusts and foundations; and companies. Each has its own characteristics for fundraisers, which I summarise below:

Government/state

- big, complex;
- the largest single source of funds for the Third Sector;
- political agenda, political timetable.

People

- the largest private sector source of funds for the Third Sector;
- divided into a wide variety of market segments;
- wealth of consumer information available;
- some donor information available.

Grant-making trusts and foundations

- established to give away money;
- dominated by a few large trusts; when 8,800 trusts were surveyed by Charities Aid Foundation (CAF) it was found that more than one-third (37%) of the total money granted comes from just 12 very large trusts (Source: *Dimensions of the Voluntary Sector*, CAF, 1998, p88);
- information available in directories.

Companies

- the weakest private sector source of funds for the Third Sector;
- plenty of information available, but not necessarily about the scale of their donations or sponsorships;
- divided into segments by legal type and by trade;
- decision takers may be specialists in community affairs, the marketing department or the boss.

A few questions to consider

Aside from the general characteristics outlined above, each of these markets has special characteristics – good and not-so-good – for you, now, in your organisation. Each market also has money, in different places at different times, and competitors who want that money.

1 What are these additional characteristics?
2 Which of these markets has money?
3 Where is it, within the market?
4 What are the big trends in the market as they concern fundraising and the not-for-profit sector
5 Who are the competition for these funds, what are their strengths and weaknesses and, critically, how much are they raising, and how much are they spending to raise it?

Jot down your answers to these questions – and welcome to the first part of your Find the Funds DIY feasibility study.

Research rigour

Before we take the next step let me suggest a few research guidelines to help you put some rigour into your study.

Markets

Use existing market research to help give your figures and ideas some backbone. Compilations for the Third Sector such as CAF's *Dimensions of the Voluntary Sector* are valuable, as are Third Sector academic studies such as those published in the *International Journal of Nonprofit and Voluntary Sector Marketing*. For business there is a huge range of often expensive reports and analyses. Ask the librarian at your regional business reference library to give you a hand, or try your local chamber of commerce. On the web, try *The Economist* (www.economist.com) and the *Financial Times* (www.ft.com). In the 'people' market try government statistics such as *Social Trends*.

Look in each of these sources for:

- big overview figures (e.g. total populations, total incomes);
- trends and predicted trends for the next three years;
- figures that affect your market: numbers of new companies moving into your region; family expenditures in the age group that interests you, and so on.

Even a few of these figures will transform your study from an interesting piece of guesswork into a report on real markets and real possibilities.

Find the Funds at home: Who cares about us?

Your **stakeholders** do. Stakeholders (see Chapter 4 *People*) are the people who have an interest in your organisation. Here are some examples:

- board members and ex-members;
- clients or users of your service;
- donors;
- employees of the organisation, ex-employees and their families;
- families of clients/users;
- government (local, regional, national);
- members;
- neighbours of the organisation;
- people in other not-for-profit organisations;
- professionals (doctors, lawyers) who advise your clients;
- suppliers (including your accountant, lawyer, bank);
- volunteers and ex-volunteers;
- your bank;
- your founders.

You can probably add to this list. Now consider;

- How many are there?
- Which of these stakeholders should be funding us?
- What might be their interest in doing so?
- What will be the impact on these stakeholders if/when we start a fundraising programme? How can we minimise any negative impact – and make the most of any positive impact?

If you are planning any type of change, from a new fundraising programme to a change of name, it is your stakeholders who will be the first to react and who may be the first to donate. The feasibility of your idea probably depends to a large extent on these reactions and donations.

The leadership question: Are we ready for fundraising?

One of the most important ingredients for a fundraising campaign is leadership. Are our leaders – our board, our executive director, our key volunteers, our senior staff – ready for a fundraising campaign? Do they want all the hassle and heartache that accompanies a campaign?

Invite a group of leaders together to discuss the ten critical questions listed below. More than five no's probably means that significant fundraising development is not feasible, at least with the present leadership.

	Yes	No
Are we: committed to the cause?		
able to ask?		
persistent?		
truthful?		
organised?		
innovative?		
Do we have contacts, or can we find them?		
Do we have a vision for the organisation?		
Does this vision need more money?		
Have we donated money, ourselves?		

(Adapted from *The Complete Fundraising Handbook*, Sam Clarke and Michael Norton)

The need

Fundraising is powered by need. We need more money to help these children. We need more money to build a better hospital. Embarking on fundraising means a lot of hard work and cost. Once you start fundraising there is no turning back; it simply isn't worth the investment. We must be absolutely certain that we have enough **need** to drive the fundraising machine.

Check your needs

- Which needs do we meet at present?
- How much money is required just to offer current services?
- What is the current level of unmet need?
- How much money would be required to grow current services to meet these needs?
- What is the estimate of future need?
- How much money is required to develop new services?
- Are these services the best way of meeting these future needs?

If answers to these questions are not readily available, you and your colleagues will need to gather together a group including board members, colleagues who provide services to clients, clients and fundraiser(s). This group will have to think big and sometimes unpleasant thoughts about the raison d'être for your organisation.

Start constructing a budget and funding targets

The work you have done on your needs provides, if you add in your administration and management costs, the expenditure part of a three-year budget.

Now go back to those two Find the Funds market studies you did earlier. Given the size of the markets, trends and key characteristics what do you anticipate will be your results in those markets?

Your budget should show for the next three years:

Main sources of income (insert here the results of your market studies)
Costs (make sure you include new projects that are planned)

Surplus or Deficit (which = total income less total costs)

Reserves at start of year
Reserves at end of year (which = Reserves at start of year plus Surplus (**or** minus Deficit))

Does your budget balance? In other words, does it keep your reserves above an agreed minimum level? If it doesn't, then go back to colleagues and discuss whether cuts in spending, or increased fundraising, are feasible and if so, under what conditions.

See? We're talking feasibility all the time!

Where are our strengths and weaknesses?

SWOT – Strengths, Weaknesses, Opportunities, Threats – is a clever way of analysing your organisation, inside and out. Don't just think about fundraising when you are completing your SWOT, think about all aspects of your work.

Look inside the organisation for strengths and weaknesses. Look outside the organisation for opportunities and threats. SWOT shows up the strengths you emphasise in fundraising and the weaknesses you should be working to correct. Opportunities and threats help you assess, subjectively, the likely risks in your plans – part of understanding how feasible they are.

	Strengths	**Weaknesses**
These are internal features of your organisation and its people:	• Well known in our area • Enthusiastic volunteer support • A track record for innovation	• Lack management time • Very little money to risk in a new fundraising venture • Dependence on only one funder
	Opportunities	**Threats**
These are features in the world outside your organisation:	• Growing demand for services in our sector • Regional economy growing fast • Government concern about service provision in our sector	• One very large national organisation in our field; could swallow us up • A future loss of public interest in our sector • A change of local government

Making and testing the case

The 'case' is the arguments we use to persuade people to support us. These will depend on the need and the audience. (The case as presented to the regional director of social welfare is quite different to the case presented to a local business club.) A case statement includes all the arguments and the figures that a potential donor needs.

Test the case

There are two phases in testing the case – internal and external. Both phases use one-to-one or group interviews as the best method. Set up interviews of about an hour with your own leadership and key staff (that's the internal phase) and with a sample of donors and non-donors (the external phase).

You can use the techniques employed by market researchers here: aim for a balanced and replicable sample of donors (e.g. by taking every nth donor in each of a number of gift bands: £10–49, £50–99, £100–500.) Amongst non-donors, aim for a balanced and replicable sample amongst the segment of the market you are aiming at. Persuading people to take part in a study takes time. It helps a lot to explain why you are doing the study, to reassure them that you will not ask them for money and that their answers will be treated in confidence.

Devise questions that will test the interviewee's interest in your organisation, her/his motives for supporting you, and to uncover her/his negative feelings about the organisation and the people who run it. For instance you might ask:

- What is your view of the social problem or need that we are trying to solve/satisfy?
- How do you think that companies/trusts/people in this region regard that social problem/need?
- Which leading organisations do you think of when I mention that social problem/need?
- What, or who, might obstruct our plans to solve/satisfy that social problem/need?
- Is ours the right organisation to tackle that social problem/need? Why?
- How do you think that our organisation is viewed by other companies/ trusts/people in this region? What do they like and what do they dislike? What is their view of our leadership and management?

For a larger study get some professional help with this part of the study; for a small or local one, make sure you try out these questions on a couple of friends first of all. Discuss the case statement during the interview, looking for participant reactions. The interviews should be recorded and a transcript typed up.

Finalise and present report

You've cracked it! Your Find the Funds feasibility study included:

- market research;
- stakeholders review;
- leadership check;
- needs analysis;
- a projected budget;
- SWOT analysis;
- checking your case.

You are now ready to present your findings to the board. Don't blow all that work away with a poor-quality presentation; go in and give them a real show (see Chapter 7 *Turning information into useable stuff*). Your report should include: key findings, analysis of case, evaluation of potential donors, recommendation on fundraising goals, assessment of leadership, a fundraising plan and a fundraising budget. They'll love it.

7

Turning information into useable stuff

Chapter objectives

▶ Learn how to collect information while promoting your cause.
▶ Understand the benefits of 'selling' researched information.
▶ Learn how to present persuasive research.

Example problems

1 'Oh no. Not a meeting with [prospective donor] Jane Goldfinger. She makes me so nervous.'
2 'I can't believe that **** Management Committee. I spent hours finding them a list of companies for us to approach, and they couldn't even be bothered to read it.'

No salespersons, please

This chapter uses one idea in two different places. The first place is that terrifying moment when you are sitting face-to-face with Jane Goldfinger, prospective donor; the time when your mouth dries up and your hands feel clammier than an August oyster. The second place is that equally awful moment when you are faced with a boardroom full of tired trustees who don't really want to read your research. But the idea at the heart of this book is that many people prefer finding out to selling. If you are a natural salesperson, able to talk the hind legs off a Spanish mule and three assistant donkeys then, please, skip this chapter.

Finding the Funds while you present – the secret of a Find the Funds pitch

Remember that even the best fundraisers have to meet three prospects to get one donation. Most of us are pretty happy if we can get one gift from every five meetings. That means that four of the meetings were wasted, doesn't it? No. It doesn't. Those meetings are often valuable sources of information. And that's the basis of this technique. Concentrate on one simple theme: finding out about those prospects. Be a real nosey Parker; you will find as I have that taking an interest in people humanises them, makes them real people, not cold distant prospects. And the more you find out the easier your fundraising will be.

Let's drop into a meeting between Sam Shybloke and Jane Goldfinger:

Sam: 'So, Ms Goldfinger . . . '

Jane: 'Do call me Jane.'

Sam: 'Well, Jane, I've been reading some of the news about Goldfinger Corporation and I would love to know more about your deal with IndiaLabs.'

Jane: 'I'm pleased you mentioned that. I was in India on holiday and met up with the president of IndiaLabs. They are the leading Indian software house . . . '

    (Jane goes on to tell the story. Sam has started. By focusing on **finding out** he has got Jane talking about a favourite subject.)

Jane: ' . . . and we signed with them only last week.'

Sam: 'Is India a big focus for your future expansion?'

Jane: 'Yes. I like the country and they like our products. '

Sam: 'It is a wonderful place. I was speaking to our field director in Delhi only last week and . . . '

Sam has started to move the interview round by mentioning his own interest in India. He will ask many more questions, but he knows that Jane is interested. If Sam is clever, he will be able to uncover Jane's interest in India, her experience with other not-for-profits, her contacts, and so on. Finally, he and she will arrive naturally at the point where, if it feels right, Sam can give Jane the chance to join in, by making a substantial gift. They will hardly notice that it happened.

By focusing on **finding out**, rather than trying to pitch up and sell Jane a product, Sam will develop a much closer relationship with Jane than he would have achieved with a 'hard-sales' approach. He takes time to understand Jane and she appreciates that.

Questions, questions

Plan your next meeting with a prospect. Start by researching them, then compile a list of the things you don't know. Remember (see Chapter 4 *People*) that you are focusing on three main areas: **connections, assets** and **motivation**. Below is a starter list of questions.

Connections

Lived in/visited the town/country we work in?

Know other doctors/social workers/[insert here the professional group you work with]?

Know anyone on the board of [insert name of a current donor trust]?

Where did you go to school, university?

Where was early training done?

Family: brothers, sisters, children?

Do you attend church/mosque/synagogue? Where?

Member of Rotary or similar?

Member of any trade bodies relevant to our organisation?

Assets

Any connections to a grant-making trust or CAF account?

Hobbies, spare-time interests?

Nature of job, position in company?

Family home, location?

Style of upbringing?

How is your company doing?

Has your trust benefited from the recent upturn in the stock exchange?

Motivation

Friends affected by our work?

Friends in our client group (e.g. people with disabilities, people in Africa, people who care for animals)?

Worked in our field/area?

What were the big influences in your childhood?

What was the most exciting thing you ever did?

Writing this list, it looks pretty intrusive. Yet when you think about the kind of conversation you have each week in the pub or the changing room, you will see that we are not only used to these kinds of questions, we actually like to be asked them, to have a chance to talk about ourselves. You will be pleasantly surprised at how much relevant, useful donor information will be revealed if you simply take an interest in your donor. This is true whether you are talking about Jane Goldfinger, Countess of Wealthing, or Jane Goldfinger, trustee of the Smallfund Trust. In the latter case Jane is an influencer, not a decider, but her views, her connections, and the trusts assets are all real targets for your Find the Funds techniques.

How to present your research

Example Problem 2 is a common complaint amongst researchers. People simply can't be bothered to wade through the research to find the nuggets hidden in the middle. Why should we bother with all this Find the Funds stuff if no-one is going to take an interest in our research?

We bother because we want to change the organisation. You may be reading this book because you want to raise enough money to pay for a new staff member; to find trusts that will support you long-term; to recruit new trustees to strengthen your board. If we want these changes to occur in our organisation, we are going to have to sell our ideas to our trustees or managers. One powerful method for doing just that is, of course, research. Research can back up our arguments with facts, with collected opinions or with an objective view. To do so, research must be well presented, and well sold. Doing so is an art.

The ART of research

Accurate

The first test for your research is accuracy. When you make that ground-breaking presentation to your trustees, make sure that you are accurate. The easiest way of doing this is to make sure that your research comes from more than one source. Just because a DSC trust guide says there are 457 trusts that support children's projects doesn't make it true. Check with the CAF directory and with CaritasData's *Top 3,000 Charities* too.

Ask a colleague to read your report to check for typos or obvious blunders (such as naming a recently deceased person as chair of a company). Get on the telephone and do a bit of amateur journalism, checking your facts where possible with the original sources, and looking for recent trends and changes.

Relevant

One of the traps that many fall into when they are presenting research is that, having found out all about the frozen food industry (or whatever), they then spend half an hour droning on about sales trends for fish fingers to their bemused audience. Don't. Edit down your wordiness, and if you can't, get a hard-nosed friend to do it for you. Would cutting 33% out of your first draft make it more focused? Yes.

Start your presentation with a clear brief (see Chapter 11 *Finding funds, losing time*). Include your brief at the start of your report, so that everyone knows what you were looking for. Don't wander off down fascinating but irrelevant research avenues. Check that each page relates closely to the brief. Be ready to politely but firmly divert irrelevant questions at your presentation.

Timely

The best time to present research is just before it is needed. Sounds obvious, but too much research is presented either too early or too late. Too early, and you risk the information changing and thus going out of date; too late and the information will not be used.

Two more tips:

- Present your research using an overhead projector whenever possible, and get used to the rigour of editing your copy down to 12 words (maximum) per transparency. Use diagrams, pictures and flip-charts to make your point succinctly.
- Put a brief executive summary at the front of any document of more than six pages.

Selling research

Those overloaded trustees in Example Problem 2 at the start of this chapter are typical of many committees and boards, not just in the not-for-profit sector. They simply can't be bothered to read your stuff. But if they don't read it, they will not act on your recommendations. They won't authorise those precious extra pounds you need to produce a new brochure for the trusts market; they won't ask their friends in the dog food industry for sponsorships, even though your research demonstrates that they should.

The research was good, we were accurate, relevant and on time. But we failed to sell them the idea. What's to be done? First, remember that research has many functions. We use research to:

- inform;
- reassure;
- persuade;
- create change.

Some of the time, research simply confirms what we know already. It **reassures** us that our charity is taking the right decisions. This is a powerful sales proposal at any trustees meeting: 'Yes, Chair, you were right to vote for the development of a new legacies campaign; our research confirms that.'

Sometimes we use research to **persuade** colleagues. Three members of your committee say no to the new legacies campaign, three say yes. The chair is undecided. Wade in with accurate, relevant, well-presented research and, likely as not, you will persuade the wrong guys of the errors of their ways. In almost every case we research to **create change** in our organisation. So you, the researcher, must move swiftly from selling research to selling change. You will have your own ideas on that process, but bear in mind the researcher's addiction to objectivity. Staying objective and above all honest is the most effective sales tool you can use.

Keeping one up the spout

One final trick for you. When you are making that presentation, perhaps working your way through a list of names that your charity might approach, do keep one or two names back. That way when Dr Rind says, 'But my dear, we can't possibly ask Mrs Rasher for money. She hasn't got a bean,' you can say, 'Thank you, Dr Rind, but I was already considering replacing Mrs Rasher on this list with Mr Spout, whose details I have here.' A few names up the spout can save your research from dying at the hands of Dr Rind.

8

Managing information

Chapter objectives

▶ Learn how to uncover knowledge in your organisation.

▶ See how to collect and manage information.

Example problems

1 'Soros? Soros? Where have I heard that name before? Wasn't he that chap who used to go out with Maureen in accounts?'

2 'My filing cabinet is so full that I can't get the door open. What should I do?'

Introduction

The problem with information is that there is too much of it. It's all around us and every day we discover more. This chapter is designed to help you work your information stock to the greatest advantage.

The research factory model

Imagine a typical car factory: outside, in the stock area, piles of metal sheet, tyres, steering wheels and airbags; inside, busy, skilled engineers and their robot friends sticking the bits together; at the factory gate, transporters taking shiny new cars to the showrooms. Your organisation is like that car factory.

What is your raw material? It is knowledge. Stuff you know about trusts or companies or people, stuff you can use to make your fundraising dreams come true. You have a stockpile of data. Your sensible factory manager knows that sheets of metal in her stockpile get rusty. So she orders stock just in time (JIT) for it to be used by the engineers and robots. You too can order your data stock JIT and I explain how, below. The stockroom manager is skilled at scouring the stockpile for the red plush seat covers needed for the new model. You can learn to scour too – scouring your office and your contacts for the type of donor you need.

The engineering team select the best production process for the particular model of car they are building. That's part of planning for research. Meanwhile the sensible manager is controlling costs by controlling the use of time, the most expensive component in any factory. Both topics are covered in Chapter 11 *Finding funds, losing time*. The design team dream up hypothetical new models. We can mimic that process to develop our own model donors as I explain under 'Prospect hypothesis' below. The car sales team are busy too, selling the finished product and getting customer feedback. We cover that aspect of management in Chapter 7 *Turning information into useable stuff*.

But let us start at the beginning – information arriving at your 'factory'.

Data as stock: stock delivery

You hear about a new prospect – a grant-making trust that is perfect for your new project. First, a rumour goes round the office; then you spot something in the press; and finally, when the new edition of the trusts directory arrives, there are the details about the trust. Information comes in like that, from word of mouth, from press cuttings and in new publications. There are ways of organising this apparently haphazard process:

Word of mouth information – using old-timers

Remember old Roger? You know, the chap with the grey hair and the false teeth who works in accounts. Been here for years. He and other long-standing staff members can give you a lot of very valuable information about donors and prospects. They remember that Peter Schlikenpot was once a student activist working for your organisation (he is now the chair of a major grant-making trust); and that Sue Lipschmaker, the well-known TV presenter, used to volunteer at the children's home you run.

Whenever you start a new fundraising programme, make sure you talk to your long-standing staff members, former volunteers and trustees to collect this valuable historical information. Using a prospect hypothesis (see below) may help this process. Peer reviews (see Chapter 4 *People*) are also useful here.

Word of mouth information – the cocktail party problem

At a cocktail party for local VIPs at the town hall you meet 'Dr, um Dr, er now what was his name? He seemed really interested in our work.' You've got the problem. Word of mouth information is so easy to lose. A simple solution is to use prospect notepads. Notepads help staff and volunteers to collect information about prospects in a quick orderly fashion. Because they are pre-addressed, they also ensure that the information gets to the right person – you.

Prospect Notepad

Completed by: On:

Event:

The following prospects or contacts were mentioned:
Name   Organisation   Mentioned by   Notes

Please return this Prospect Notepad in a sealed envelope marked HIGHLY
CONFIDENTIAL to [you] at [your organisation].

Print off a few hundred, postcard-sized, and ensure that each of your trustees,
key volunteers and colleagues has a supply. After the cocktail party, film première
or drinks at the pub, your contact simply fills in the notepad, returning it to you
by post or pigeon-hole. That way, precious information is collected immediately.
Better communication, better co-ordination and better targeting of prospects are
just some of the advantages of this system.

Press cuttings

If you work for a leading NGO you will probably have a press cuttings agency. If
you don't, there is another simple way of collecting press information about
prospects. You pay the subscription of a magazine, and a volunteer, keen to read
the magazine, clips it for you. For example, a yachting enthusiast clips *Yachting
Monthly* for a fundraiser who wants to target the yachting industry and the
people who buy the big yachts. You can make the same offer to your volunteers
or friends to collect information in almost any market, from antiques to zoology.
Make sure that your volunteer clipping team is well briefed and kept up to date
on new prospects and projects.

Data as stock: storage

Paper and electronic filing

To ensure that you find what you need quickly, files should be classified using the
function–activity–transaction system. To do this, break down your job into its
major components, each of which is called a function. Break each function down
into sub-sections called activities, and, if necessary into sub-sub-sections called
transactions.

If, for instance, your job includes:

- marketing;
- personnel management;
- legal compliance;

then these should be the functions that govern your filing system. Within each function there are a series of activities. Here is a selection:

- Marketing – management;
- Marketing – fundraising;
- Marketing – press relations;
- Personnel management – recruitment;
- Personnel management – reviews;
- Personnel management – disciplinary procedure;
- Legal compliance – charity registration;
- Legal compliance – insurance;
- Legal compliance – accounting.

If we focus on those marketing activities we can see various transactions:

- Marketing – management – planning group meetings
- Marketing – management – feasibility study
- Marketing – management – budgets
- Marketing – fundraising – research
- Marketing – fundraising – prospects in development
- Marketing – fundraising – publicity/fundraising literature
- Marketing – fundraising – individual donors (A-Z)

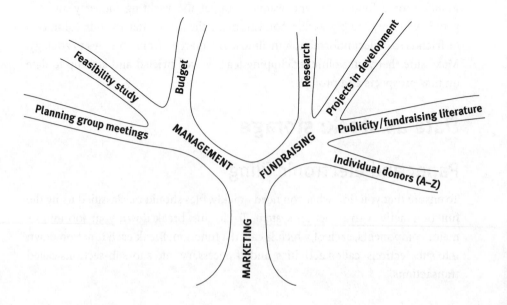

The advantage of a tree filing system like this is that it grows (and can be pruned) with your job. Take on a new function, and you simply insert a file series with that function name into your filing cabinet or computer. Delete an activity from your job description and you can archive those files. Remember to keep just one series of files on individual prospects (by family name from Mrs Aardvark to Mr Zbignew). Don't be tempted to allow two fundraisers to stock two sets of individual files; you will only cause duplication and lack of co-ordination.

Throwing out files

Yes, you can, and tell your admin manager that I said you could. Don't be tempted to keep all files forever. Aim to keep information on living people, but a file on a trust with whom you haven't had a relationship for five or more years is pretty well useless. And worse, those useless files clog up your information system. They take up filing space and, naturally, you are tempted to consult them when you are busy finding the funds. You don't have time, so remove the temptation by bunging them in the recycling bin.

Cautionary notes:

- You do have a statutory duty to retain certain files; please don't recycle these. Bear in mind the principles of the Data Protection Act, featured in Chapter 10 *Clean secrets*.
- Do ensure that your recycling is secure, preferably shredded across the type-line (e.g. vertically down this page).
- Keep old files on significant donors; they can be very useful for targeting wealthy families with a history of giving to the organisation.

A fundraising library

If you really want to be the fount of all knowledge, build up a good fundraising library. Refer to Chapter 2 *Let's get started* for some ideas. The advantage of having a fundraising library next to your desk is that everyone comes to your bit of the office when they are looking for new funds. That will help you co-ordinate funding approaches because you get to hear when two of your colleagues both come to look up the same corporate sponsor. Make sure that everything in your library is clearly labelled 'For Reference Only' and keep any really valuable stuff locked in a drawer, especially your back copies of *Hello!* magazine.

JIT data management

The JIT idea is that you get in information just in time, not months beforehand. Applying this to your work you might, for example, delay researching a couple of companies until a fortnight before they are to be approached; research done earlier than that risks going out of date before the company is contacted. Similarly, don't rent lists or commission outside research until you are sure that you are ready for it.

Scouring the stockpile: knowledge scouring

Knowledge scouring – otherwise known as 'how to search your best friend's in-tray' – is based on the idea that information ends up, in most organisations, in all the wrong places. To Find the Funds you must uncover it. But how? The information is often so well hidden – in old files, in-trays, the director's head – that people don't even know which questions to ask, let alone where to find the answers.

Let us uncover it in a methodical way. First, draw up two or three prospect hypotheses (see 'New models: prospect hypotheses' below) for your campaign. That means you know who you are looking for. Now list all the places where information is kept in your organisation – database, filing cabinets, the press office, your best friend's deep in-tray. Look at my knowledge scouring check sheet in the Appendix and add places that are particular to your organisation.

Then start scouring your office, using the check sheet given in the Appendix. You will be amazed at the results. You will find, as I have, unconnected databases all holding information about prospects; an unused consultant's report listing important people known to the organisation; a VIP list held by the press officer; and a campaigning department stuffed full of information and contacts with companies, all of them useful prospects for your next fundraising campaign.

New models: prospect hypothesis

A car designer spends a lot of time thinking about potential customers before she puts pen to paper, or mouse to pad. You can do the same – developing your dream donor from what you know already. (The metaphor only goes so far; it is not yet possible to build dream donors from sheet metal and plastic.)

You create a theoretical – hypothetical – prospect by combining your own knowledge of the types of people who donate at present (young, female, professionals living in the north east, or whoever is your donor group) with any market research you have either commissioned or can purchase (*Dimensions of the Voluntary Sector* might be a starting point). You then take a blank profile of the sort laid out in the Appendix and start to fill in as many of the spaces as you can.

Do this exercise two or three times, producing a different prospect hypothesis each time. The more precise you can honestly be, the better. Your finished prospect hypotheses will be an enormous help, focusing your research work, encouraging your colleagues and trustees to suggest people who more-or-less match the hypothesis, and guiding your knowledge scouring. The prospect hypothesis is the core of a good briefing for external researchers too.

Be the factory manager

Think about your organisation as an information factory. Ensure that information flows from the supplier to the user as quickly as possible. Keep your stockpile tidy and fresh. Create new types of prospect and donor. Do all this and Finding the Funds will become a cost-effective, efficient process.

9

Finders keepers

Chapter objectives

▶ Understand key skills required of researchers.
▶ Learn how to manage outside suppliers such as research agencies.

Example problem

'Lovely book, Chris, but who actually does this research? Me? You've got to be joking.'

Introduction

It is everyone's responsibility to find the information that leads to funds: yours, your trustees, your volunteers and if possible the responsibility also of the people your organisation works with. Get them all involved and your fundraising will benefit enormously. But someone has to co-ordinate and manage all that funder information. That someone might be a volunteer, a staff member or an agency.

Volunteers

Some organisations use volunteers to co-ordinate their research and information. It can suit volunteers to have a steady, thought-provoking job. Using volunteers means that you save on costs – but do please allow time for supervision, and some expenditure on directories, copying, telephone and travel. Volunteer researchers can lose motivation rapidly because they are not in the frontline of your organisation's work. So make sure that you involve them in your decision taking and, above all, that you feed back to them the fundraising results of their research work.

Staff

Your options here are probably to allocate a percentage of an existing staff member's time to research or to employ a new full-time or part-time person. Consider these points:

- Skills and aptitudes are vital to research. Sloppy or untimely work will be especially apparent, and especially awful, in a researcher.
- There are economies of scale in research because the amount of bought-in information (such as directories) that you need for four researchers is about the same as the amount you need for one. Similarly, one hour of work per week will get you some information, but you will get 20 times as much for just 10 times as many hours.
- The supply of **experienced** fundraising researchers in the UK is tiny. Consider re-training someone with library or journalism skills. The Institute of Charity Fundraising Managers (ICFM) and some research suppliers offer this type of training.
- Demand for research is likely to be heaviest at the start of and a little way into any new appeal. Plan for this, either by allocating extra time or by hiring in short-term agency help at these peak times.
- Use the research plan featured in Chapter 11 *Finding funds, losing time* to help estimate your likely staffing needs.

Skills required

Finding the funds takes special skills. Here is a selection of relevant skills suggested by the US Association of Professional Researchers for Advancement (APRA). For the full list, visit their website at www.aprahome.org

Knowledge of:

- donor types – individual, corporate, foundation and government;
- ethics statements by APRA, ICFM, the Council for Advancement and Support of Education and other appropriate associations;
- your organisation's mission, history, programmes, goals and philosophy;
- your organisation's record-keeping systems.

Understanding of:

- the role information plays in prospect development;
- relevant information and how to analyse data;
- the fundraising process;
- the motivations behind charitable giving.

Proficiency in:

- locating relevant information in a variety of formats, including hard copy, telephone calls, online and conversations with staff and volunteers;
- writing clearly and concisely;
- appropriate management of confidential information;

- recognition of wealth indicators;
- basic file maintenance;
- communicating effectively with diverse audiences, and in listening skills.

That's a long list, but it's only part of the full skill set for experienced researchers. If you are considering using a researcher then take a look at the original list before putting together a job description.

Using suppliers

Like everything, research suppliers have their pros and cons. The big suppliers are the vendors of data (see *Sources list*). Here we will deal with the research agencies that are listed in any copy of ICFM's *Who's Who in Fundraising*.

Agencies offer:

- an outside and independent view – important if you are faced with a difficult or contentious decision;
- the capacity for larger studies – useful at the points in your appeal when you experience a high level of demand for research, typically about a quarter of the way along;
- reassurance for your trustees that research is being handled professionally by people who have done plenty of research before;
- anonymity – which can be useful if you want to research trusts or companies without them knowing who you are;
- an established set of professional ethics and rules. All reputable agencies should be able to show you their code of conduct – typically from either the Market Research Society, ICFM or APRA.

Specialist agencies probably use a wider range of sources than you can get your hands on; and they take the risk and responsibility for the job. Finally, of course, you don't have to do the work!

All this comes at a cost and there are other points you should consider that may weigh against the use of agencies:

- Data confidentiality – your data may have to go out of house to the agency for analysis. What security and confidentiality systems do they have?
- Agencies may not fully understand your needs; after all they haven't been living with them for the last few years.
- You don't control the research process when it is being done by an agency. They might say or do something you don't approve of.
- Agencies can be a short-term solution to a long-term need. It might be better to sort out your own research department.

You can control some of this by contract. Use your research brief (see Chapter 11 *Finding funds, losing time* to start the process off, meet the agency to discuss the project, ask for a clear, detailed quote, and then negotiate a contract that you can both live with.

Finding an agency

ICFM's *Who's Who in Fundraising* is the key source. Market research agencies are listed by the Market Research Society (which has data on agencies, with information on sectors and specialisms) and the website of the British Market Research Association (see *Sources list*). For freelance researchers contact the National Union of Journalists or ASLIB, the Association for Information Management.

10

Clean secrets

Chapter objectives

▶ Learn how to differentiate your information by its level of confidentiality.
▶ Understand the ethical limits of research.

> **Example problem**
> 'My boss says it's OK to take donor files home for the weekend. I'm not so sure.'

Introduction

This is the honesty chapter. In it I show how to grade information so that the truly confidential stuff is protected and I discuss the ethics of research. Note that research into donor ethics is covered briefly in Chapter 5 *Companies*.

Confidentiality

Fundraising depends on trust. Donors will only open their hearts and their cheque books if they trust you. Your fundraising committee will entrust you with their contacts only when they trust that you will not pass on this personal data to others. We must demonstrate again and again that we are worthy of those confidences. We can do so by developing and using a confidentiality policy, by collecting just the information we need, and by staying within the law.

A confidentiality policy

I don't want to turn your office into a KGB bunker, all passwords and secret codes; most organisations should regard most of their information as publicly available. But some information is confidential – partly because the law says so and partly because you have a duty to your donors and prospects to keep it that way. A confidentiality policy helps you decide which files are confidential, which are not.

It is helpful to divide information into three types:

- public domain;
- confidential;
- personal and highly confidential.

Public domain

Any document that a member of the public could obtain simply by requesting or purchasing it (e.g. a press cutting, a company annual report, a who's who book) is in the public domain. These documents may be freely exchanged, bearing in mind only the laws of copyright.

Confidential

Documents that relate to your organisation's management, strategy or finances would be typically regarded as confidential. They are confidential in the sense of commercial confidence; leaking them might result in damage to the organisation.

Your policy should cover the receipt, storage, distribution and destruction of confidential information. For example, you might specify that you will keep confidential documents in files that are locked during prolonged staff absence and, if they are on computer, that are protected by a password known to all staff. Confidential documents would normally be destroyed by shredding or disk formatting.

Highly confidential

The test for highly confidential is: does this document contain information about a living person? Any document containing the name of a donor, supporter or prospect should be treated as highly confidential. Again, your policy should cover receipt, storage, distribution and destruction. Here are some examples;

'Paper documents will be stored in a locked filing cabinet with three keyholders: the campaign manager, the fundraiser and the chair of the trustees. These documents may be seen only with the permission of a keyholder. They may be copied only with the written permission of a keyholder. They may be faxed to a keyholder or a user authorised by a keyholder at a direct line fax, but never to a general open-office fax.'

'Highly confidential document drafts will be destroyed by secure shredding as soon as they are updated/redrafted.'

'Highly confidential electronic documents will be protected with a password known only to the three keyholders. The password will be changed monthly.'

'Highly confidential computer files should be unavailable to other users of the computer network. They should be backed up by a keyholder only, with the backup disks/tapes being held at a safe location off-site from our organisation.'

Mixed files

Mixed files (including for example a prospect profile, an internal report and a set of press cuttings) should be classified at the level of the most confidential document they contain. Do bear in mind that the Data Protection Act covers non-computerised as well as computerised personal records.

Computer replacement

Don't forget confidentiality when you replace that aged PC. Any computer containing confidential material must have its hard disk re-formatted before it is sold or passed on.

Where confidentiality is broken

Work out what you will do if a computer is stolen or a highly confidential file goes missing. Specify who should be told and within what timeframe.

Staying within the law

This book is not a tome on the Data Protection Act 1998 (for details of the act see DSC's *Data Protection for Voluntary Organisations*). It is your job to ensure that you and your organisation work within the act. You should be aware of two pieces of legislation that affect anyone doing research: copyright and data protection.

Copyright law allows a certain amount of copying for non-commercial purposes, but it completely prohibits you from copying chunks of information either onto paper or disk. For a good overview, see *Copyright for Library and Information Science Professionals*, ASLIB.

Data protection legislation, the subject of continuing discussions both in the UK and at the EU, protects the individual 'data subject' from abuse of data relating to her or him. Registered data controllers (i.e. you) must comply with the data protection principles in relation to the personal data they hold. The principles state that personal data shall be:

- obtained and processed fairly and lawfully;
- held only for lawful purposes which are described in the register entry;

- used or disclosed only for those or compatible purposes;
- adequate, relevant and not excessive in relation to the purpose for which they are held;
- accurate and, where necessary, kept up to date;
- held no longer than is necessary for the purpose for which they are held;
- able to allow individuals to access information held about them and where appropriate correct or erase it. Data subjects are now entitled to a description of the data being processed, a description of the purposes for which it is being processed, a description of any potential recipients of her/his data and except in limited circumstances, any information as to the source of her/his data;
- surrounded by proper security. Note that the act states explicitly what precautions data controllers must take.

Note that this legislation covers data held not only in computers, but also in manual filing systems. Especially strict conditions apply to the processing of sensitive data such as information relating to racial or ethnic origin, political opinions, religious or other beliefs, trade union membership, health, sex life and criminal convictions. The explicit consent of the individual data subject will usually have to be obtained before this sensitive data can be processed unless the controller can show that the processing is necessary based on one of a defined set of criteria.

The Data Protection Commissioner is keen to help charities to live within the law. When in doubt about whether what you are proposing is within the law get on the phone and talk to them. Contact them at www.dataprotection.gov.uk/dprhome.htm for updated information and a set of guidelines. Bear in mind that data protection law will evolve as cases are tried through the courts. What you believe to be legal today may be illegal tomorrow.

The ethics of research

All this research is terribly intrusive isn't it? Should we peer into people's private lives? These questions don't have a clear yes or no answer. The response depends on who's peering, why and how they are peering, and precisely what they are peering at.

Who's peering?

You have the right like any member of the public to collect public domain information from Companies House, *Who's Who*, DSC's trusts directories or any one of the hundreds of other sources open to the public. But the minute you start finding the funds you are likely to go a lot further than that. A trustee will mention a conversation she had with a local businesswoman; it sounds as though this woman's business is going very well and she is known to have an interest in our work. You are now dealing with information that is not public domain: rumour, private stories, personal confidences, subjective opinions.

Who you are is important at this point. You, the sensible employee or volunteer for a solid not-for-profit organisation? That's fine, so long as you stick to good working practices. You, the trustee's personal friend who, over a beer later that evening spills the beans to two other mates? No, not within the ethical frontier. Of course you and I are both these things. We're sensible employees, and we're people with friends, with whom we share secrets. But when it comes to personal donor or prospect information, we must be the worker, not the gossipy friend.

Why and how are you peering?

As the Association of Professional Researchers for Advancement (APRA) statement below makes clear, the **method** of research affects the ethics of the research. Devious methods are rightly outlawed by APRA. The **motive** behind the research is important. Only research the information you really need, and only do so when the fundraising campaign justifies it. Aside from the ethical considerations, researching like this is much more efficient.

Precisely what are you looking at?

We saw in Chapter 4 *People* that a great deal of personal information can be uncovered simply by relying on public sources. There are other sources – credit-checking agencies, eavesdropping, unauthorised tape-recording, long-range photography, burglary – but these are strictly for spooks and Scotland Yard.

A recurring theme for some fundraisers is the question of client records. You're fundraising for a hospital or a medical charity; why shouldn't you take a look at patient or client records? After all, Oxford University can look at its student record, so why can't you look at your hospital's patient database? I'm afraid that here we are dealing with Hippocrates. The oath in his name, taken by all medics, requires that patient information is kept confidential:

> 'Whatever I see or hear in connection with my professional practice or not, in the life of men, which should not be made public, I will not divulge, considering that all such knowledge should remain secret.'

It's someone else's ethic but one that I, for one, am happy with. Would you want anyone other than your doctor and you to see your patient information? No thanks.

If you want a good measure of what is OK and what is not try this test, suggested by Dr Alison Binns at the Open University: 'Imagine the data subject standing behind you as you are keying information about her into your database. If that thought makes you feel uncomfortable, then you should not be keying the data.'

The APRA Statement of Ethics

This document gives a clear set of guidelines and best practice in research, which I have summarised here. For the unedited original version, visit www.aprahome.org

APRA members shall support and further the individual's fundamental right to privacy and protect the confidential information of their institutions. APRA members are committed to the ethical collection and use of information. Members shall follow all applicable laws as well as institutional policies governing the collection, use, maintenance, and dissemination of information in the pursuit of the missions of their institutions. APRA members shall respect all people and organisations.

Prospect researchers must balance the needs of their institutions to collect, analyse, record, maintain, use, and disseminate information with an individual's right to privacy. This balance is not always easy to maintain. The following ethical principles apply, and practice is built on these principles:

I Fundamental principles

Confidentiality

Confidential information about constituents (donors and non-donors), as well as confidential information on the institutions, is protected so that the relationship of trust between the constituent and the institution is upheld.

Accuracy

Prospect researchers shall record all data accurately. Such information shall include attribution. Analysis and products of data analysis should be without personal prejudices or biases.

Relevance

Prospect researchers shall seek and record only information that is relevant and appropriate to the fund-raising effort of the institutions that employ them.

Accountability

Prospect researchers shall accept responsibility for their actions and shall operate in a professional manner, accountable to their institutions and to the constituents who place their trust in prospect researchers and their institutions.

Honesty

Prospect researchers shall be truthful with regard to their identity and purpose and the identity of their institution during the course of their work.

II Suggested practice

Collection

1 The collection of information shall be done lawfully, respecting applicable laws and institutional policies.
2 Information sought and recorded includes all data that can be verified and attributed, as well as constituent information that is self-reported (via correspondence, surveys, questionnaires, and so on).
3 When requesting information in person or by telephone, it is recommended in most cases that neither individual nor institutional identity shall be concealed. Written requests for public information shall be made on institutional stationery clearly identifying the inquirer.
4 Whenever possible, payments for public records shall be made through the institution.
5 Prospect researchers shall apply the same standards for electronic information that they currently use in evaluating and verifying print media.

Recording and maintenance

1 Researchers shall state information in an objective and factual manner; note attribution and date of collection; and clearly identify analysis.
2 Constituent information on paper, electronic, magnetic or other media shall be stored securely to prevent access by unauthorised persons.
3 Special protection shall be afforded all giving records pertaining to anonymous donors.
4 Electronic or paper documents pertaining to constituents shall be irreversibly disposed of when no longer needed.

Use and distribution

1 Researchers shall adhere to all applicable laws, as well as to institutional policies, regarding the use and distribution of confidential constituent information.
2 Constituent information is the property of the institution for which it was collected and shall not be given to persons other than those who are involved with the cultivation or solicitation effort or those who need that information in the performance of their duties for that institution.
3 Constituent information for one institution shall not be taken to another institution.
4 Research documents containing constituent information that is to be used outside research offices shall be clearly marked **confidential**.

5 Vendors, consultants, and other external entities shall understand and agree to comply with the institution's confidentiality policies before gaining access to institutional data.

6 Only publicly available information shall be shared with colleagues at other institutions as a professional courtesy.

III Recommendations

1 Prospect researchers shall urge their institutions to develop written policies based upon applicable laws and these policies should define what information shall be gathered, recorded and maintained, and to whom and under what conditions the information can be released.

2 Prospect researchers shall urge the development of written policies at their institutions defining who may authorise access to prospect files and under what conditions.

3 Prospect researchers shall strongly urge their development colleagues to abide by this code of ethics and these fundamental principles.

11

Finding funds, losing time

Chapter objectives

▶ Discover three management tools for research.
▶ Understand the four ingredients of a good research brief.
▶ Learn how to make your boss a better person.

> **Example problems**
> 1 'There is too much to do! I have no time for research! Help!'
> 2 'My boss has just asked me to find everything I can on Paul McCartney, by Friday!'

Introduction

Don't panic. These are common problems for researchers and there are treatments that will help even the most desperate cases. Most of these treatments are based on common sense. Some are more radical. But the focus of all of them is time. Manage your time and you will manage your research – however horrifying your in-tray.

Managing time

Here are four easy steps to help you manage your research time better:

1 Consider each research job, however small, as a distinct research project. Keep all the papers relating to it in one file.
2 Write a brief for each research project.
3 Prepare a research plan for each project.
4 Keep a research diary for each project.

Let's look at steps 2–4 in detail.

Research brief

Why are briefs important? Because they define in clear, practical language precisely what you are looking for. If the language doesn't look clear or practical then you probably need to clarify your thinking and re-write your brief.

A brief contains four ingredients;

- background;
- objectives;
- outputs;
- constraints.

The **background** to the research project explains why we need the research, for example:

'We're launching a new minibus service to help wheelchair users in our smaller county towns to get to arts events in larger cities. The service will cost £50,000 to start up'.

Objectives should be clear and precise, for example:

'The research should identify 25 grant-making foundations each capable of making a gift of £5,000 or more. **All** foundations in your report should have made at least one gift of this amount or more in the last two years.

We must be able to show for **all** foundations that their policies, track record or future direction include **any of** the following: rural issues, transport or physical disabilities. **All** should have funded cultural activities in the past two years.'

Outputs means the final research product. Here you identify the information you really need and when you need it. Talk to all the potential users of your research and find out how it is to be used. Do we need a three-page profile or would half a page do? For example:

'Report the research in two phases. In the initial report include:

- foundation name;
- location town;
- income and the year figures relate to;
- total grant-making and the year figures relate to;
- examples of grants of £5,000 or more;
- notes on policy or preferences.

On the basis of this report, a second, in-depth report by [date] will focus on 10 foundations showing:

- address, telephone, fax, e-mail, website;

- financial information for the latest three years;
- board members, desk officers, director (full names, confirmed by telephone);
- all known recipients of grants in excess of £1,000 over last two years;
- notes from your interviews with desk officers on future policy directions;
- your analysis of each foundation against our fundraising programme.'

Get the idea? Once we start to think about how the research is going to be used we can do it in stages and report it in a consistent format, and so save time.

Constraints are not as unpleasant as they sound, but simply the old business of time and money. For example, you may know that you have to send off your applications within the next three months, that your organisation can't afford to have more than one person working on this particular job, and that your travel budget for the year is £300. You may also have ethical or geographical constraints. For example:

'Complete the research within one month of the go-ahead. Remember that we do not work with foundations whose main source of income is the tobacco industry. All identified foundations should be based in the north of England.'

Now you have it; the perfect brief. Try using it next time you want to research some prospects.

Research plan

You have probably used a similar action plan in other contexts. Essentially, it chops up tasks into their component parts so that we can sensibly estimate time and cost. An example of the type of research plan we use at The Factary appears in the Appendix; feel free to use it in your own organisation.

You use the columns as follows:

Action	a list of all the steps you must complete to do the project (visit the library, buy a copy of *Who's Who*)
Complete by date	the dates by which you must complete each action
Hours	how many hours you estimate each action will require
Extra costs	any additional costs (materials, phone, travel) that you will incur in completing that action.

Add up the hours, allow for a 20% slippage in your estimate, and convert the time into research time costs. This normally means multiplying your hours by a set figure representing your wages plus your share of overhead costs. Add in the extra costs analysed under travel, database, phone and materials. The final total cost is the sum of research time cost plus extra costs.

Now you can evaluate your research against the likely fundraising outcomes and take sensible decisions about how much time and money to spend. You will avoid falling into the trap of spending £2,500 of your time to raise £1,000 of funding

Research diary

The research diary is a record of what actually happened. In that sense it should, ideally, reflect what you put into your research plan. An example of blank research diary for you to copy and use appears in the Appendix.

This time you use the columns as follows:

Name	you!
Date	today's date
Hours	the number of hours actually spent doing the job
Research notes	a note of what you did today for this research project
Extra costs	any additional costs you incurred

Your growing store of research diaries will help you estimate how long jobs will take next time. Your research diary is also a security measure for your colleagues, telling them what has been completed when you disappear on a surprise holiday or come down with 'flu for a fortnight.

Retraining the boss

Why do fundraising bosses continue to ask their researchers to 'find everything you can on Paul McCartney' (a true-life case, folks) or sack their four-person research team at the start of a £70m appeal only to discover, two-thirds of the way through the appeal, that they have run out of prospects (yes, also true)? It's because they just don't understand research, isn't it?

So let's retrain the boss. Show her what good research can do, and what it can't. Have her spend two days being a researcher so she finds out that it takes more than 10 minutes to 'knock up some notes on George Soros'. Above all, train the boss in briefing for research and planning for research (see above). She will come to understand that research is a serious business that requires time, commitment and rigour.

Conclusions

Let's do that one more time

This book set out to answer the 'Where is the money?' question that all fundraisers ask. I promised you a book not about how to fundraise but about how to find the funds. I hope you feel that these objectives have been met. We have worked through each of the key fundraising markets, describing sources and methods in detail. I have discussed management of information, presentations and the ways in which you can 'sell' information to colleagues. And we have looked at special-interest topics such as feasibility studies and confidentiality.

Big ideas

Running throughout the book has been one theme: that research does more than simply find you a page-full of facts. Research can actually help you become a wonderful fundraiser. This is not some hair-brained marketing slogan. It's the result of doing real-life research for unwilling fundraisers. These fundraisers don't want to ask that company for money because it's embarrassing and difficult and probably only-just-ethical, and anyway the directors are snooty toffs who wouldn't give me the time of day.

But with a little research we find out that director X has a personal interest that links strongly to our own. We find that she is a normal human being with the normal range of good and awful in her life – and it becomes easier to talk to her and Find the Funds from her company.

Time management

Have I mentioned this before? Probably a hundred times, if you had the time to count them. Time is the fundamental measure of research productivity, and the most expensive resource you will use. Managing time by using the planning and recording techniques I describe in Chapter 11 *Finding funds, losing time* is essential. Without these simple techniques your research will run off the rails (or run so far down them as to miss the point).

Information management

You may not have thought of yourself as a manager before, but that's what you are, whoever you are, when it comes to information. Information and knowledge are your most valuable resources. They deserve the best management. My model, explained in Chapter 8 *Managing information*, is to treat information as solid, tangible stock with a value and a shelf-life. Your job is to use that stock to help you find the funds.

Managing your information stockpile means knowing what you have – reviewing your databases and those of colleagues, checking those filing cabinets at the back of the third floor, and scouring your information for knowledge. Managing information also implies that you take careful, well-judged decisions about what information to buy and what to borrow. So go on, appoint yourself Information Manager in Chief, and inform your fundraising.

Reality check

Does all this finding the funds stuff really work? Er, yes. Years of doing research for fundraisers in Britain, and years of persuading them of the value of research have shown me that a little knowledge makes an enormous difference:

- The 'great and good' fundraising committee at a Midlands university who said that they couldn't possibly approach their friends for money because, well, you know old chap it's all so, um, difficult. We researched the committee members and found their contacts (see Chapter 4 *People* for the techniques). Presented, nicely, with a list of people we-knew-they-knew, the committee suddenly gained confidence and went on to Find the Funds – from the very contacts they had said they didn't have.
- The tiny educational charity with one member of staff who did everything from type the minutes to organise the events. Didn't like fundraising, not one bit. So we found her a grant-making trust with a trustee who had written an article about a daughter with a condition that was relevant to the educational charity. Staff person gets interested, writes to the trustee and wins the substantial and long-lasting support of the grant-making trust.
- Or the three Giorgios. The fundraiser for an animal charity visits Canada to campaign against the seal cull. On the ferry he meets three Italian men all called Giorgio. One Giorgio arrived in his own helicopter and is clearly very wealthy. Tragically, our fundraiser forgets rich Giorgio's surname. The Factary's sleuth team is asked to find the right Giorgio. We find him, after a lot of frustrating research, when he and his helicopter are found listed amongst the VIPs in the web pages of a swish Sicilian restaurant. Fundraiser and donor get together for a happy ending.

Yes, finding the funds techniques work in real-life fundraising situations. Try them and see for yourself.

Crystal balls

Where is fundraising research heading? It's still such a new profession in the UK that it is hard to predict trends with any precision. But here are a few of the futures I can see:

Clever computers

The eternal discussions about the best database for fundraising will continue to blow through the sector, with software houses vying for pole position. (I have not entered that debate here, first because anything I write today will be hopelessly out of date by the time it is in print and second because the choice of supplier probably depends more on who you trust than on bells and whistles in the software.)

It is apparent, though, that increasingly sophisticated information management tools are becoming available. These allow you to store your data in a variety of different formats with a software tool that digs into the data warehouse to extract the specifics you want. Cleverer computers like this will allow you to mix data from buy-in databases with files, your own databases and records, giving you a much more complete understanding of your donors' relationships with you.

More data

This is part of a general trend toward more data. Data on consumers, corporates and trusts, is all much more accessible than it was even a year ago and this trend will continue for years to come. This strengthens the case for just-in-time data management, for which I argue in Chapter 8 *Managing information*. Don't buy a directory this year unless you really need it; next year it will be bigger and better.

Better market data

A few years ago there wasn't an academic in Britain that was seriously studying the Third Sector. The Charities Aid Foundation led the way with its surveys of fundraising and donating, and now academics are setting up research centres specifically focused on Third Sector activities. We can expect to see more of these in future, both in the UK and in Europe. This information is valuable. It gives you the opportunity, easily and at low cost, to measure your fundraising performance against others. It will also show you gaps in the market, people who are not being attracted as supporters by other not-for-profits.

Information overload

The flipside of better computers and more data is that it gets easier to drown in information. Now that we can easily source so much biographic and corporate data on many individuals, we can easily lose ourselves in pages and pages of irrelevant waffle. Get cynical, get critical, get tough with colleagues or, if you are desperate, buy an alarm clock and limit yourself to no more than four hours to research each prospect.

The research professional

UK fundraisers are beginning to get serious about research. Larger not-for-profits and middle-sized organisations are employing their own researchers or using research suppliers (see Chapter 9 *Finders keepers*). The fundraising research professional is being born.

These professionals are in short supply; ICFM's Research in Fundraising special interest group reckons there are about 80 full-time prospect researchers in the UK. In the future we can expect more people to join the profession and more structure (professional training and qualifications). That will be good for everyone concerned.

Knowledge

The big change in research will appear so stealthily that you won't even notice it happening. One minute you'll be telling colleagues to 'collect information' and the next you'll be talking to them about 'understanding knowledge'. Knowledge is not just the new buzzword of the information community, it is a better way of thinking about our organisations. Knowledge is the accumulation of information, history and contacts held throughout our organisation – from the volunteer in Upton to the chairman in Downham. Understanding our knowledge means working inside the organisation to collect the huge range of information it contains. It's hard work but it pays huge dividends, because it turns an unused resource into valuable fuel for fundraising, management and development.

Feedback, please

This book is not directly connected to the web, but it's only a modem away. So go on, plug in and send me an e-mail. I want your feedback. Tell me what you think of the book and the ideas it presents, what you found useful, what you didn't. And if you do find a useful source of information on trusts, companies, people or government, let me know (and I might even send you one I have found). E-mail me now at carnie_jarrett@compuserve.com

Thank you

Thanks for sticking with me to the end. If you have read the whole book up to this point then award yourself the Find the Funds Gold Medal for Perseverance. If you are reading this bit in the bookshop to see how the story ends then stop cheating and buy me now.

Sources list

All titles in this list published by the Charities Aid Foundation (CAF) or the Directory of Social Change (DSC) are available from DSC Books, 24 Stephenson Way, London NW1 2DP. Call 020 7209 5151 for a free publications list. Prices were correct at time of going to press but may be subject to change.

Sources on trusts and foundations

CAF NGO Books
Charities Aid Foundation
www.ngobooks.org.uk
Online book shop for not-for-profit sector. Sales point for CAF publications.

CAF Online
Charities Aid Foundation
www.cafonline.org
Regular news bulletins and case studies about CAF's work.

The CD-ROM Trusts Guide
Directory of Social Change, 1999, £129.25 (inc. VAT)
Updated annually. UK charitable trusts from A Guide to the Major Trusts and Guides to Local Trusts. Search by geographic area, trusts' interests.

Charitable Trust Reports Service
Smee & Ford Ltd
St George's House,
195-203 Waterloo Road,
London SE1 8XJ.
Tel 020 7928 4050,
Fax 020 7928 5837
E-mail smee@compuserve.com

Reports on money left in wills either to create a charitable trust or to substantially add to a trust. Around 40–50 reports each year (out of 280,000 wills). Cover Great Britain.

Charity Commission: Central Register
Charity Commission for England and Wales
Harmsworth House,
13-15 Bouverie Street,
London EC4Y 8DP
Tel 0870 333 0123
www.charity-commission.gov.uk
Register contains names, trustees and financial information on foundations and trusts. Website allows searches in the register by name, number, keyword (including objects) and area of operation.

Charitynet
Charities Aid Foundation
www.charitynet.org
Links to other foundation sites. Can't identify specific foundations for you.

Datatrust
Arts Council of Scotland
12 Manor Place,
Edinburgh EH3 7DD
Tel 0131 226 6051
E-mail help.desk.sac@artsfb.org.uk

Free database of 360 Scottish trusts and funds including policy, eligibility (individuals, charities), some financial information, no trustees. Free service.

Directory of Grant Making Trusts Focus Series: Rural Conservation and Animal Welfare; Children and Youth; Schools, Colleges and Educational Establishments; International; Social Care; Older People; Manchester, Liverpool and the North West; Yorkshire, Humberside and the North East; Cambridgeshire, Norfolk and the East Midlands
Charities Aid Foundation,
1997, 1998, 1999 £19.95 (Rural Conservation £24.95)
Subsets of CAF's Directory of Grant Making Trusts database designed for specific groups.

The Directory of Grant Making Trusts Vol. 1–3
Charities Aid Foundation, 1999,
£89.95
Directory of over 3,500 trusts including contact and grant making information. Vol. 3 gives detailed research into largest 250 trusts.

Directory of Scottish Grant Making Trusts
Scottish Council for Voluntary Organisations (SCVO), 1999
18-19 Claremont Crescent,
Edinburgh EH7 4QD
Tel 0131 556 3882,
Fax 0131 556 0279
Directory of approximately 550 grant-making trusts in Scotland, showing contact details, policy, restrictions, date established. Available on paper and disk.

The Directory of Smaller Grant Making Trusts
Charities Aid Foundation,
1999, £29.95
Directory of 1,000 smaller grant-making trusts including contact and grant making information.

The Educational Grants Directory
Sarah Harland, Directory of Social Change, 1998, £18.95 (new edition available September 2000)
Educational charities which support children and students up to first degree level.

FunderFinder
Available via Councils for Voluntary Service and via the website
www.funderfinder.org.uk
Software for searching for grants from trusts and companies for organisations and individuals.

Funding Digest
RTI Publications
Suite 1.02,
St Mary's Centre,
Oystershell Lane,
Newcastle upon Tyne NE4 5QS
Tel 0191 232 6942,
Fax 0191 232 6936
www.rtipub.co.uk
Funding information for the UK. Includes quarterly supplement on new trusts.

Funding for Voluntary Action
Northern Ireland Voluntary Trust,
Belfast
Tel 028 9024 5927
Free directory of grant-making trusts in Northern Ireland.

Fundsnet
Fundsnet Services Online

419 Inmaculada Street,
San Juan
Puerto Rico 00915-1234
E-mail webmail@Fundsnet Services
www.fundsnetservices.com
*General philanthropy site including
directories of foundations.*

Grantseeker CD-ROM

Charities Aid Foundation, 1998,
£58.69 for renewable subscription
*CAF's Directory of Grant Making
Trusts in CD-ROM format. Allows
searches by name, interest, trustee
name and location. Was six-monthly,
but subscribers to Release 3 (March
2000) will have access to the data for
one year, until March 2001.*

A Guide to Grants for Individuals in Need

Sarah Harland, Directory of Social
Change, 1998, £18.95 (new edition
available September 2000)
*Details of over 2,100 charities
concerned with individual poverty.*

A Guide to Local Trusts

Sarah Harland, Louise Walker,
Directory of Social Change, 1999,
£17.95
*Four editions: Greater London,
Midlands, North of England, South of
England. Total over 2000 grant-
making trusts and foundations.*

A Guide to the Major Trusts Vol. 1, 2 and 3

Luke FitzHerbert et al,
Directory of Social Change,
biennial, £19.95
*Vol. 1 contains 300 UK trusts with
grant information, contact details,
exclusions and a diary of trustee
meetings. Vol. 2 covers next 700 trusts.
All have a potential to give £50,000 or
more. Vol. 3 covers another 400 trusts,
plus trusts in Northern Ireland,
Scotland and Wales.*

Guide to the National Lottery Charities Board

Luke FitzHerbert, Directory of Social
Change, 2000, £15
*Includes annotated NLCB grant
assessment manual.*

New Trust Update

The Factary
The Coach House,
2 Upper York St,
Bristol BS2 8QN
Tel 0117 924 0663
Fax 0117 944 6262
E-mail TheFactary@compuserve.com
*Comprehensive monthly report on
newly registered grant-making trusts.*

Philanthropy in Europe

C/Girona 18,
E-08461 St Esteve de Palau,
Barcelona,
Spain
Tel +34 93 848 14 16
Fax +34 93 848 16 20
E-mail carnie_jarrett@
compuserve.com
*Bi-monthly report on foundations and
philanthropy in Europe.*

Poptel

Poptel
90 De Beauvoir Road,
London N1 4EN
Tel 020 7923 9465
Fax 020 7254 1102
www.poptel.org.uk
Online supplier. Includes not-for-profit

*news, legal information and a
corporate responsibility database.
Poptel offers access to Dialog and FT
Profile services.*

Scottish Charities Office

FICO (Scotland)
Trinity Park House,
South Trinity Road,
Edinburgh EH5 3SD
Tel 0131 551 8127
*The source of information about
Scottish grant-making trusts. Index of
Charities is open to the public; shows
name, address, last contact name, last
contact date.*

SectorNet

Northern Ireland Council for
Voluntary Action (NICVA)
127 Ormeau Road,
Belfast BT7 1SH
Tel 01232 321224,
Fax 01232 438350
E-mail info@nicva.org
www.nicva.org
*Details on more than 6,000 not-for-
profits in Northern Ireland and the
border counties of the Republic of
Ireland, in a searchable database.*

Social Directory

Bryson House
28 Bedford Street,
Belfast BT1 7EP
Tel 028 9032 5835
*Directory including a range of
Northern Ireland local groups that
provide support and self-help on
health and social welfare matters.*

Top 1000 Charities in Scotland

Alan Rattigan, CaritasData Ltd,
annual, £95

Kemp House,
152-160 City Road,
London EC1V 2NP
Tel 020 7250 1777 Fax 020 7250 3050
E-mail info@caritasdata.co.uk
www.caritasdata.co.uk
*Name, financial and contact
information on 1,000 not-for-profits in
Scotland. Executive and trustee names,
professional advisers and rankings.
Includes a who's who in Scottish
Charities. Available in book form only.*

Top 3,000 Charities (The Baring Asset Management Top 3,000 Charities)

Alan Rattigan, CaritasData Ltd,
annual, £80
Kemp House, 152-160 City Road,
London EC1V 2NP
Tel 020 7250 1777,
Fax 020 7250 3050
E-mail info@caritasdata.co.uk
www.caritasdata.co.uk
*Name, financial and contact
information on 3,000 non-profits in
the UK. Executive and trustee names,
professional advisers and rankings.
Available as book or CD (see Top
10,000 Charities).*

The Top 10,000 Charities on CD-ROM

Alan Rattigan, CaritasData Ltd,
quarterly, £350-£750 (standard or
professional versions)
Kemp House, 152-160 City Road,
London EC1V 2NP
Tel 020 7250 1777,
Fax 020 7250 3050
E-mail info@caritasdata.co.uk
www.caritasdata.co.uk
Name, financial, trustee and contact

information on not-for-profits in the UK. Searchable by activities, location, grant-making status, expenditure and people. Includes information on UK quoted companies and their charity giving.

Trust Monitor
Directory of Social Change, three issues per year, £30
Policy changes and news on top trusts. New trusts.

The Voluntary Agencies Directory
NCVO, London, 1999, £22.50
Regent's Wharf,
8 All Saints Street,
London N1 9RL
Tel 020 7713 6161,
Fax 020 7713 6300
www.vois.org.uk/ncvo/
Over 2,500 UK voluntary organisations including contact details.

Sources on companies

Advertisers Annual: The blue book
Hollis Directories Ltd, annual, £175
Harlequin House,
7 High Street,
Teddington,
Middx TW11 8EY
Tel 020 8977 7711,
Fax 020 8977 1133
E-mail orders@hollis-pr.co.uk
www.hollis-pr.co.uk
Advertising agencies, advertisers, brand names.

BRAD
Emap Business Communication

33-39 Bowling Green Lane,
London EC1R 0DA
Tel 020 7505 8000
www.brad.co.uk
Advertising agencies, advertisers, brand names. Searchable on their website BRADnet.

Britain's Top Privately Owned Companies
Jordan Publishing Ltd
21 St Thomas Street,
Bristol BS1 6JS
Tel 0117 923 0600,
Fax 0117 925 0486
E-mail
ryoung@jordanpublishing.co.uk,
www.jordanpublishing.co.uk
Unquoted UK companies with rankings by turnover.

Campaign
Haymarket Marketing Publications
174 Hammersmith Road,
London W6 7JP
Tel 020 7413 4036,
Fax 020 7413 4507
Weekly news and articles covering advertising and communications.

CD-ROM Company Giving Guide
Directory of Social Change, 2000, £99.88 (inc. VAT)
Updated annually. Company data from The Guide to UK Company Giving. Allows searches by geographical location, business, names of directors, subsidiaries, fields of support and well-known brands.

Chambers Directory
Chambers and Partners, London, annual
www.chambersandpartners.com

Website with solicitors and barristers for the UK. Lists more than 3,500 solicitors, with regional reviews and ranking by size.

City Business Library
1 Brewers Hall Garden,
London EC2
Tel 020 7638 8215
A fabulous range of corporate and people information.

Companies House
Companies House
21 Bloomsbury Street,
London WC1B 3XD
Tel 0345 573 991
also in Leeds:
Companies House
25 Queen Street,
Leeds LS1 2TW
Tel 0113 233 8338,
Fax 0113 233 8335
and in Wales:
Companies House
Crown Way,
Cardiff CF4 3UZ
Tel 029 2038 0917,
Fax 029 2038 0679
www.companies-house.gov.uk/
Filings on paper, microfiche and computer on UK companies. The original source of UK company information.

Companies House Direct
Companies House
21 Bloomsbury Street,
London WC1B 3XD
Tel 0345 573 991
www.companies-house.gov.uk/
Online service for searching company information including directors and finances.

The Company Guide
Hemmington-Scott Publishing,
quarterly, £149.50 per annum
City Innovation Centre
26-31 Whiskin Street,
London EC1R 0JD
Tel 020 7278 7769,
Fax 020 7278 9808
E-mail Webmaster@hemscott.co.uk
www.hemscott.com
Financials and facts about 2,300 UK stockmarket companies.

Corporate Citizen
Directory of Social Change, three issues per year, £30 for voluntary organisations, £55 for others.
Comments and case studies on corporate philanthropy in the UK. Identifies new sources of corporate support. Annual listing of top 100 corporate donors.

Corporate Register (The Price Waterhouse Coopers Corporate Register)
Hemmington-Scott Publishing,
quarterly £195 per annum
City Innovation Centre
26-31 Whiskin Street,
London EC1R 0JD
Tel 020 7278 7769,
Fax 020 7278 9808
E-mail Webmaster@hemscott.co.uk
www.hemscott.com
Financials, directors and advisers of UK stockmarket companies. Includes biographic information and shareholdings. Also available as CD-ROM.

D&B MarketPlace UK
Dun & Bradstreet

High Wycombe,
Bucks HP12 4UL
Tel 01494 422299
www.dunandbrad.co.uk
CD-ROM directory of UK companies.

DASH

Dun & Bradstreet, quarterly £4,000
High Wycombe,
Bucks HP12 4UL
Tel 01494 422299 or 0161 228 6543
www.dunandbrad.co.uk
CD-ROM of major shareholders,
directors of UK companies. Shows
share issue prices. Can be searched
geographically and by name.

Directory of Directors

Bowker Saur, annual, £225
Windsor Court,
East Grinstead
W Sussex RH19 1XA
Tel 01342 326972,
Fax 01342 335612
E-mail custserv@bowker-saur.co.uk
www.bowker-saur.co.uk
UK directors and their board
appointments. Includes biographic
information.

Directory of Multinationals

John Stopford, Macmillan Press Ltd,
1992
Houndmills,
Basingstoke RG21 6XS
E-mail books@macmillan.co.uk
Detailed profiles of 428 multinationals
including financials, history, notes and
major shareholders.

The Economist

25 St James's Street,
London SW1A 1HG
www.economist.com
Weekly magazine.

EIRIS

Ethical Investment Research Service
80-84 Bondway,
London SW8 1SF
Tel 020 7840 5700
www.eiris.org
EIRIS was set up in 1983 with the help
of churches and charities that had
investments and needed a research
organisation to help them put their
principles into practice. EIRIS provides
independent research into corporate
behaviour and helps charities and
other investors identify appropriate
companies.

E. M. Directory: Commercial and Social Directory of the African, Asian and Caribbean Communities in Britain

Arif Ali, Hansib, 1993
139 Fonthill Rd,
London N4 3HF
Who's who and business directory.

Expoguide

www.expoguide.com/
Information about trade shows,
exhibitions and conferences.

Financial Times

London
www.ft.com/
UK's leading financial newspaper.
Searchable archives online. Includes
online ordering of annual reports for
UK plcs at
www.FT.com/newspaper/2176.htm

FT Profile

Financial Times Information
Tel 020 7825 8000
www.info.ft.com
Online news database. Comprehensive

coverage of UK national and regional press specialist magazines and trade press. Full text coverage of all UK-quoted company annual reports.

Gifts In Kind UK
PO Box 140,
4 St Dunstan's Hill,
London EC3R 5HB
Tel 020 7204 5003

The Guide to UK Company Giving
Directory of Social Change, 2000, £25
Basic company guide, published annually.

Hollis Sponsorship and Donations Yearbook
Hollis Directories Ltd, annual £97.50
Harlequin House,
7 High Street,
Teddington,
Middlesex TW11 8EL
Tel 020 8977 7711,
Fax 020 8977 1133
E-mail: orders@hollis-pr.co.uk
www.hollis-pr.co.uk
Lists of sponsors, agencies, sponsor-seeking organisations.

Hollis UK Press and Public Relations Annual
Hollis Directories Ltd, annual, £92.50
Harlequin House,
7 High Street,
Teddington,
Middx TW11 8EY
Tel 020 8977 7711,
Fax 020 8977 1133
E-mail orders@hollis-pr.co.uk
www.hollis-pr.co.uk
Directory of PR consultancies and people.

ICC Information Ltd
Field House,
72 Oldfield Road,
Hampton,
Middx TW12 2HQ
Tel 0800 783 4045
E-mail marketing@icc.co.uk
www.icc.co.uk
A supplier of online and CD-ROM information about UK and international companies. Their Juniper online service includes 5.3 million UK limited companies, sole traders and partnerships, and over 8 million directorships.

Incomes Data Services
77 Bastwick Street,
London EC1V 3TT
Tel 020 7250 3434,
Fax 020 7608 0949
www.incomesdata.co.uk/
Information and reports about salaries for directors and others.

The Institute of Chartered Accountants in England and Wales: Directory of Firms
Macmillan Press Ltd, annual, £75
Houndmills,
Basingstoke RG21 6XS
E-mail books@macmillan.co.uk
www.macmillan.co.uk
Directory of accountancy firms.

Investors Chronicle A–Z of Investment
C Sefton, Pitman Publishing, 1996
128 Long Acre,
London WC2E 9AN
Tel 020 7447 2000,
Fax 020 7240 5771
Explanation of key terms for investors.

Useful for understanding company terminology.

Kelly's

Reed Information Services
Windsor Court,
East Grinstead House,
East Grinstead,
W Sussex RH19 1XO
Tel 01342 335866
www.reedinfo.co.uk
Directory of companies by postal address. Online version available.

Key British Enterprises

Dun & Bradstreet
High Wycombe,
Bucks HP12 4UL
Tel 01494 422299
www.dunandbrad.co.uk
Available as book and as CD-ROM; covers the UK's largest 50,000 businesses by turnover. CD-ROM covering up to 200,000 businesses is updated quarterly.

Kompass

Reed Information Services
Windsor Court,
East Grinstead House,
East Grinstead,
W Sussex RH19 1XO
Tel 01342 335866
www.kompass.com
Brand name for a variety of business directories based on listings of products. Reed publish various Kompass directories including Kompass CD Plus, Kompass Online, UK Kompass Resiter Products and Services and Company Information (vol. 1 and 2) and UK Kompass Regional Sales.

Labour Research magazine

Labour Party
John Smith House,
150 Walworth Road,
London SE17 1JT
Tel 020 7277 3346,
Fax 020 7277 3555
Magazine covering social issues. Includes exposes of British industry and wealth.

Macmillan's Unquoted Companies

Macmillan Press Ltd, annual £360
Houndmills,
Basingstoke RG21 6XS
E-mail books@macmillan.co.uk
www.macmillan.co.uk
Financial and market profiles on 20,000 unquoted UK companies

Major UK Companies Handbook

Financial Times Information (Extel Financial), twice yearly £115
Fitzroy House,
13–17 Epworth Street,
London EC2A 4DL
Tel 020 7825 8000,
Fax 020 7608 2032
E-mail rupert.hunting@ft.com
www.info.ft.com
Financial information on 850 quoted UK companies including directors, registered addresses.

Marketing Week

St Giles House,
50 Poland Street,
London W1V 4AX
Tel 020 7439 4222,
Fax 020 7439 9669
www.marketing-week.co.uk
Weekly magazine for marketing management.

PR Week
Haymarket Marketing Publications
174 Hammersmith Road,
London W6 7JP
Tel 020 7413 4520,
Fax 020 7413 4509
*Weekly news and features on the
world of public relations.*

ReedBase
Reed Information Services
Windsor Court,
East Grinstead House,
East Grinstead,
W Sussex RH19 1XO
Tel 01342 335866
www.reedinfo.co.uk
*Information from Kompass, Kelly's
Directory, Dial Industry and Directory
of Directors. 1.3m companies world-
wide are profiled, of which 200,000 are
in the UK. In addition all 1.5m
companies from Companies House are
detailed.*

Smaller UK Companies Handbook
Financial Times Information (Extel
Financial), annual £200
Fitzroy House,
13–17 Epworth Street,
London EC2A 4DL
Tel 020 7825 8000,
Fax 020 7608 2032
E-mail rupert.hunting@ft.com
www.info.ft.com
*Financial information on 1,500
smaller quoted UK companies.*

**Tuckers' Directory of the
Accountants 500**
Tuckers Directories
363 Palatine Road,
Manchester M22 4FY
Tel 0161 945 5775

*Accountancy firms including a top
500, with lists of partners.*

**Tuckers' Directory of the
Surveyors 500**
Tuckers Directories, 1994/5
363 Palatine Road,
Manchester M22 4FY
Tel 0161 945 5775
*Surveyors' firms including a top 500,
with lists of partners.*

UK Equities Direct
Hemmington-Scott Publishing
City Innovation Centre,
26–31 Whiskin Street,
London EC1R 0JD
Tel: 020 7278 7769,
Fax 020 7278 9808
E-mail Webmaster@hemscott.co.uk
www.hemscott.co.uk/index.htm
*Share prices, summarised accounts,
trading outlook, share capital for UK
quoted companies.*

Who Owns Whom
Dun & Bradstreet
High Wycombe,
Bucks HP12 4UL
Tel 01494 422299
www.dunandbrad.co.uk
*Two-volume directory showing
companies and their subsidiaries.
Available as CD-ROM.*

Willings Press Guide
Nesta Hollis, Hollis Directories Ltd,
annual £287.95 (CD ROM)
Harlequin House,
7 High Street,
Teddington,
Middx TW11 8EY
Tel 020 8977 7711,
Fax 020 8977 1133

E-mail orders@hollis-pr.co.uk
www.hollis-pr.co.uk
Details on 30,000 national and regional magazines and newspapers including trade press. International volume available.

World Guide to Trade Associations
Michael Zils, K G Saur
Ortlerstrasse 8,
D-81373 Munich
Germany
Tel +49 89 769020
www.saur.de
Trade and some not-for-profit groups in the world.

Yellow Pages
British Telecom,
London
www.yell.co.uk
Online version of yellow pages using same classification system. Shows company name, address and phone numbers.

Sources on people

Asian Digest
Hansib
139 Fonthill Rd,
London N4 3HF
Monthly magazine on the Asian community in the UK.

Asian Times
Ethnic Media Group
1st Floor,
148 Cambridge Heath Road,
London E1 5QJ
Tel 020 7702 8012,
Fax 020 7702 7937
Weekly, news stories articles and features on Britain's Asian community.

Asian Who's Who International
Asian Observer
Tel 020 8550 3745

Bar Directory
Sweet & Maxwell and the General Council of the Bar, London
www.smlawpub.co.uk
Directory also available as searchable website of UK Barristers.

Burke's Peerage and Baronetage
Charles Mosley, Fitzroy Dearborn Publishers, 1999, £295
310 Regent Street,
London W1R 5AJ
Tel 020 7636 6627,
Fax 020 7636 6982
E-mail
post@fitzroydearborn.demon.co.uk
www.fitzroydearborn.com
Reference book on UK aristocracy.

Business Age
Adrian Lithgow, Priori Publishing Ltd, monthly
1st Floor,
60 Wharf Road,
London N1 7SF
Tel 020 7490 8411,
Fax 020 7490 8422
www.businessage.uk.com
People in business with a focus on the UK.

City of London Directory and Livery Companies Guide
City Press, annual, £22
42 North Station Road,
Colchester CO1 1RB
Tel 01206 545121,
Fax 01206 545190
Livery (trade) companies in London. Names and home addresses.

Complete Peerage
Sutton Publishing Ltd, 1987, £95
Phoenix Mill,
Thrupp,
Stroud,
Gloucestershire GL5 2BU
Tel 01453 731 114,
Fax 01453 731 117
E-mail sales@sutton-publishing.co.uk
www.bookshop.co.uk/sutton
Now a little aged, one-off publication on the aristocracy.

Debrett's Peerage and Baronetage
Charles Kidd, Macmillan Press Ltd,
every five years: 2000, 2005, £500
Houndmills,
Basingstoke RG21 6XS
E-mail books@macmillan.co.uk
www.macmillan.co.uk
Genealogical and biographical reference book on Britain's aristocracy and royal family. Website is not searchable.

Directory of Members
Chartered Assoc of Certified
Accountants, annual
29 Lincoln's Inn Fields,
London WC2A 3EE
Vol. 1 list of members: full name, home address, year of graduation. Vol. 2 practising members and firms.

Dod's Parliamentary Companion
Vacher Dod Publishing Ltd, annual,
£105
PO Box 3700,
Westminster,
London SW1E 5NP
Tel 020 7828 7256,
Fax 020 7828 7269
E-mail politics@vacherdod.co.uk
www.vacherdod.co.uk
The structure and people of the UK parliament including biographic entries for MPs.

Eastern Eye
Southnews plc
148 Cambridge Heath Road,
London E1 5QJ
Tel 020 7702 8012
www.southnews.co.uk
Publish an annual Asian Rich List compiled by Dr Philip Beresford.

Estates Gazette Interactive
Estates Gazette, London, monthly
www.egi.co.uk
Property service: database of UK property market including deals, who's who, company information, commercial properties available. Subscription only, but free trial month. Part of Reed Business publishing.

Five Hundred Notable Women
American Biographical Institute,
Raleigh, USA, 1998
Biographic information on women.

Forbes Richest People
Forbes Inc, annual, US$13.99
www.forbes.com
Bios and features on the 400 richest people in the world.

Foremost Women of the Twentieth Century
International Biographical Centre,
1998 (currently out of print)
Cambridge CB2 3QP
Biographies of living and dead women.

Halliwell's Who's Who in the Movies
John Walker, HarperCollins, London,
1999
Movie and cinema who's who.

Havers' Companion to the Bar
Havers Directories Ltd
Rowling House,
Rowling Goodnestone,
Canterbury CT3 1QB
Tel 01304 813727
Barristers directory.

International Dictionary of Films and Filmmakers
Nicholas Thomas, Gale Research
835 Penobscot Bldng,
Detroit MI 48226-4094
Tel +1 313 961 2242,
Fax +1 313 961 6815
www.gale.com
Detailed biographies of writers, actors, directors living and dead.

International Who's Who in Music and Musicians Directory
David Cummings,
International Biographical Centre,
Cambridge CB2 3QP
Biographies of 8,000 living classical and light classical musicians.

The International Who's Who of Women
Europa, London, 1992
Biographic directory.

The Jewish Year Book
Stephen Massil, Vallentine Mitchell through Frank Cass Publishers,
annual, £26
Newbury House,
890–900 Eastern Avenue,
Ilford,
Essex IG2 7HH
Tel 020 8599 8866,
Fax 020 8599 0984
E-mail info@frankcass.com
www.frankcass.com

Listing of leading people and institutions in the UK Jewish community.

Land Registry
www.open.gov.uk/landreg/home.htm
Information about services and Property Price Report.

National Directory of Black Women's Organisations
1996
Winchester House,
9 Cranmer Road,
London SW9 6EJ
Women's organisations in the UK.

News Update
National Alliance of Women's Organisations
Suite 44,
Diamond House,
37–38 Hatton Garden,
London EC1N 8EB
Monthly source of information on women's organisations in the UK.

People of Today
Debrett's Peerage Ltd,
73/77 Britannia Rd,
London SW6 2JY
www.debretts.co.uk
A who's who with a more modern feel than Who's Who from A & C Black. Also available on CD ROM. Debrett's offer an ancestry tracing service.

Pride of Black British Women
Deborah King, Hansib, 1995
139 Fonthill Rd,
London N4 3HF
Biographic information about leading black British women.

Probate Department of the Principal Registry of the Family Division
First Avenue House,
42–49 High Holborn,
London WC1V 6NP
Tel 020 7936 7000
Wills and estates; formerly at Somerset House. Copies of wills may be viewed here (or ordered from regional offices).

The Sunday Times Rich List
Philip Beresford, *The Sunday Times*,
London
www.sunday-times.co.uk
Annual survey of Britain's rich, appearing in April. Includes rankings of rich people in various businesses, and regional rankings. Searchable at the website; look for the April editions of The Sunday Times.

Third World Impact
Arif Ali, Hansib, 1996
139 Fonthill Rd,
London N4 3HF
Who's who and useful articles on leading people from ethnic minorities in sports, society, business, etc.

UK Register of Expert Witnesses
JS Publications, 1993
Tel 01638 561590
Experts in various fields, indexed by field.

Vacher's Parliamentary Companion
Vacher Dod Publishing Ltd, quarterly,
£9.50
PO Box 3700,
Westminster,
London SW1E 5NP
Tel 020 7828 7256,
Fax 020 7828 7269

E-mail politics@vacherdod.co.uk,
www.vacherdod.co.uk
Peers, members, officials, select committees, senior civil servants, executive agencies, national organisations, high court, diplomats and ombudsmen.

Wealth Register
Philip Beresford, Esco Business Services, 1997, £25
Robjohns Farm,
Vicarage Road,
Finchingfield,
Braintree
Essex CM7 4LJ
Tel 01371 810433
Biographic information on 5,000 wealthy people in the UK.

Wealth Watch
Sunrise Publications
Lanet Farmhouse,
Lanivet,
Bodmin PL30 5J
www.wealthwatch.co.uk
Monthly report on the rich in the UK. Includes useful profiles and news.

Who's Who
A & C Black
35 Bedford Row,
London WC1R 4JH
The establishment who's who for the UK. Also available in CD ROM including historic information.

Who's Who in Charity
Alan Rattigan, CaritasData Ltd, 1999
Kemp House, 152–160 City Road,
London EC1V 2NP
Tel 020 7250 1777,
Fax 020 7250 3050
E-mail info@caritasdata.co.uk

www.caritasdata.co.uk
Name and biographic information on trustees, presidents, patrons and staff of people listed in Top 3,000 Charities.

Who's Who in Fundraising
Institute of Charity Fundraising Managers (ICFM), annual
Market Towers, 1 Nine Elms Lane, London SW8 5NQ
Tel 020 7627 3436,
Fax 020 7627 3508
Listing of ICFM members and supplier companies; available to members only.

Who's Who in Greater Manchester
Manchester Literary & Philosophical Publications Ltd
Tel 0161 228 3638,
Fax 0161 228 3571
man.litphil@virgin.net
Regional biographic directory. Last edition published 1996 and unlikely to be another.

Who's Who in Scotland
Carrick Media, 1999
2/1 Galt House,
31 Bank St,
Irvine KA12 0LL
Tel 01294 311322
National biographic directory.

The World Who's Who of Women
Ernest Kay, International Biographical Centre, 1994
Cambridge CB2 3QP
Biographic directory.

Writers' and Artists' Yearbook
A & C Black
35 Bedford Row,
London WC1R 4JH

Annual directory of publishers, literary agents, publishing and finance for writers and artists.

Sources on government and state funding

A Guide to Funding from Government Departments and Agencies
Susan Forrester, Directory of Social Change, 1998, £18.95
Funding from over 200 sources in the UK including advice on how to raise it.

Civil Service Yearbook
www.civil-service.co.uk
Searchable on the web.

Directory of International Funding Organisations
Charities Aid Foundation, 1997, £9.95
United Nations and other international pan-governmental organisations.

The Environmental Funding Guide
Susan Forrester, Directory of Social Change, 1998, £16.95
National Lottery, government, EU, trusts, companies, competitions as sources of funding.

Funding Opportunities for NGOs
British Overseas NGOs for Development (BOND)
Regent's Wharf,
8 All Saints St,
London N1 9RL
Tel 020 7837 8344,
www.bond.org.uk
Government and private sector funding for NGOS.

Guide to Libraries and Information Units in Government Departments and other Organisations
P Dale, British Library, 1998, £37

The Vacher Dod House of Commons Companion
Vacher Dod Publishing Ltd, 1998, £90
PO Box 3700,
Westminster,
London SW1E 5NP
Tel 020 7828 7256,
Fax 020 7828 7269
E-mail politics@vacherdod.co.uk
www.vacherdod.co.uk
The structure and people of the UK parliament.

Vacher's European Companion
Vacher Dod Publishing Ltd, £15.50
PO Box 3700,
Westminster,
London SW1E 5NP
Tel 020 7828 7256,
Fax 020 7828 7269
E-mail politics@vacherdod.co.uk
www.vacherdod.co.uk
The structure and people of the European parliament.

Wide-ranging UK sources

ASLIB, The Association for Information Management
Staple Hall,
Stone House Court,
London EC3A 7PB
Tel 020 7903 0000,
Fax 020 7903 0011
E-mail aslib@aslib.co.uk
www.aslib.co.uk

Association promoting best practice in information management. 2,000 corporate members in 70 countries.

British Market Research Association
16 Creighton Avenue,
London N10 1NU
Tel 020 8444 3692,
Fax 020 8883 9953
www.bmra.org.uk
Website contains information on market research agencies in the UK and allows searches against your criteria.

The Complete Fundraising Handbook
Sam Clarke and Michael Norton,
Directory of Social Change, 1997,
£14.95
Useful guide to fundraising techniques.

Copyright for Library and Information Service Professionals
Paul Pedley, ASLIB, 1998, £13.50
Staple Hall,
Stone House Court,
London EC3A 7PB
Tel 020 7903 0000,
Fax 020 7903 0011
E-mail aslib@aslib.co.uk
www.aslib.co.uk
Practical advice on dealing with current issues in copyright.

Copyright Licensing Agency
www.cla.co.uk
Advice and information on copyright law and practice.

Data Protection for Voluntary Organisations
Paul Ticher, Directory of Social Change, £12.95, 2000

A guide to the 1998 Data Protection Act.

Dimensions 2000
Cathy Pharoah and Jeremy Vincent,
Charities Aid Foundation, 2000, Vol. 1
£10, Vol. 2 £12, Vol. 3 £25,
Vols 1–3 £32.50
*Statistical analysis of figures and
trends in the UK voluntary sector.
Useful ranking tables and market
overviews. Vol. 1 covers local authority
funding, Vol. 2 the top 500 fundraising
charities, and Vol. 3 the pattern of
grantmaking by trusts and
foundations.*

Dimensions Online
Charities Aid Foundation
www.CAFonline.org/research
Additional data available free online.

Electronic Telegraph
The Daily Telegraph, London
www.telegraph.co.uk/ Newspaper
Searchable archives.

The Factary
The Coach House,
2 Upper York Street,
Bristol BS2 8QN
Tel 0117 924 0663,
Fax 0117 944 6262
E-mail TheFactary@compuserve.com
Research agency for fundraisers.

Fundraising UK Website
Howard Lake,
Fundraising UK Ltd,
36 Palestine Grove,
London SW19 2QN
Tel 020 8640 5233
E-mail hlake@fundraising.co.uk
www.fundraising.co.uk
*Central website source of links and
news on fundraising in the UK.*

Guardian On-Line
Guardian Newspapers, London
www.guardianunlimited.co.uk
*Includes The Guardian and The
Observer news services.*

National Union of Journalists
NUJ, London
www.gn.apc.org/media/nuj.html
*Source of information about freelance
researchers.*

The Sunday Times
PO Box 496,
London E1 9XN
Tel 020 7782 5000,
Fax 020 7782 5046
www.the-times.co.uk
*Website includes searchable archives
and link to The Times.*

Teach Yourself Fund Raising
Tony Elischer, Hodder & Stoughton,
1995
*Fundraising techniques in an easy-to-
read format.*

The Times
PO Box 496,
London E1 9XN
Tel 020 7782 5000,
Fax 020 7782 5046
www.the-times.co.uk
*Newspaper with searchable archives
and link to The Sunday Times.*

Wide-ranging sources: world-wide

AltaVista
www.altavista.digital.com
Internet search engine.

The Dialog Corporation
The Dialog Corporation
Tel 020 7930 5503
www.dialog.com
Online data supplier covering most business and news topics. Includes news, directories, analysts' reports, trade journals, specialist newsletters. Includes UK government and EC press releases, handbooks, encyclopaedias, corporate affiliations, Marquis Who's Who (US), Foundation Directory and Grants Index (US), Dun & Bradstreet.

Excite
www.excite.com
Internet search engine.

International Journal of Nonprofit and Voluntary Sector Marketing
Henry Stewart Publications
Museum House,
25 Museum Street,
London WC1A 1JT
Tel 020 7323 2916,
Fax 020 7323 2918
www.henrystewart.co.uk
Quarterly, academic studies of fundraising and marketing in voluntary organisations.

Northern Light
www.northernlight.com
Internet search engine which includes the text of newspapers and magazines.

Targeting the Powerful: International Prospect Research
Vanessa Hack, ASLIB, 1996
Staple Hall,
Stone House Court,
London EC3A 7PB
Tel 020 7903 0000,
Fax 020 7903 0011
E-mail aslib@aslib.co.uk
www.aslib.co.uk
Covers international prospect research including detailed lists of sources and commentaries.

Yahoo!
www.yahoo.com
Internet search engine.

Appendix: Photocopiable charts

Who are your stakeholders?

Stakeholders	Number	Have they money or other assets?	Why do they care about your organisation?

© The Factary 2000

Company profile

Company name	
President	
Chief executive	
Company HQ address	
Telephone	
Fax	
Website	
Key products	
Main markets[1]	
Turnover, last three years	
Net pre-tax profits, last three years	
Past donations to our organisation	
Other known connections between the company and our organisation	
Date researched	
Sources used[2]	
Source limitations[3]	
Researcher's name	

[1] The places where the company sells its goods. The trade press is a good source of this information.

[2] The books, directories and people you consulted.

[3] Remember to record any limitations or cautions about your sources; an out of date directory, or an unconfirmed source.

© The Factary 2000

Prospect hypothesis

Date of birth (range)	
Gender	
Home location	
Work location	
Birthplace	
Education	
Career background	
Industry sector	
Current job	
Philanthropic interests	
Political interests	
Memberships	
History with our organisation	
Family background	
Current family	
Contacts/known to	
Religion	
Cultural/ethnic background	
Possible motivations for this campaign	
Other comments	

© The Factary 2000

Knowledge scouring check sheet

We are looking for:

Hypothesis 1: _____

Hypothesis 2: _____

Scoured by: _____

Date:

Sites:	Database	Filing cabinets	Press office	In-trays	Other: _____
Information found Notes:					

The Factary Research Plan

Project:			
Plan Prepared by:		**Date:**	

ACTION	COMPLETE BY DATE	HOURS	EXTRA COSTS
Subtotal			
Margin 20% (slippage)			
Total Hours			
Research Time Cost			
Travel			
Database			
Phone			
Materials			
Final Total			

© The Factary 2000

The Factary Research Diary

Name of Project _____   Report Due Date _____

Name	Date	Hours	Research Notes	Extra Costs

Total Hours: ☐   **Total Extra Costs:** ☐

© The Factary 2000

Index